And she was a CHRISTIAN

Why Do Believers Commit Suicide? ✝

Peter Preus

NORTHWESTERN PUBLISHING HOUSE
Milwaukee, Wisconsin

Third printing,   2013
Second printing, 2012

Art Director: Karen Knutson
Designer: Pamela Dunn

Northwestern Publishing House
1250 N. 113th St., Milwaukee, WI 53226-3284
www.nph.net
© 2011 by Northwestern Publishing House
Published 2011
Printed in the United States of America
ISBN 978-0-8100-2343-7

CONTENTS

Part Five
Gospel Relief for the Hopeless (Especially for Pastors) ....

PREFACE

When Christian families grieve, they seek encouragement and support from Holy Scripture. That's also true when a loved one dies from suicide. What is unique to suicide survivors is the added burden of a piercing question articulated by society. Did this family member die in the faith? A follow-up question is voiced by the one grieving. "If he did lose his faith, shall I, the surviving spouse, parent, child, or sibling, be held responsible somehow?" If survivors were taught once upon a time that all suicides go to hell, they may in fact ask themselves: "Did I help my beloved down that path?"

It is a time, unlike any other, when a family needs Christian comfort and support. Unfortunately, another question, which often confronts family members following a suicide, is whether the pastor will conduct a funeral for their loved one. As in former centuries, pastors have shown a reluctance to minister to the grieving in any beneficial way. The mind-set reads something like this: "We can't say that suicides go to heaven or that suicide is a forgivable sin. By doing so, we might give somebody who's entertaining the thought of taking his life the excuse he's looking for." So there evidently is little or nothing we can say either privately or publicly that will console the grieving survivors. We must simply keep quiet about the matter. The church is engaged in a conspiracy of silence, and it is our apparent duty to prolong the silence.

It may be argued that the stigma associated with suicide has been removed to a large extent in recent years but with little help from those in the church. The general public has become better informed about depression and mental illness and their association with suicide. More people have come to accept the truth that suicide does not result from having come from a bad family. It isn't merely a case of avoiding the issue. Suicide is psychological. There is a very definite connection between mental illness or depression and suicide.

Nevertheless, there are a couple of trends that continue to generate ignorance about suicide. The first is evident in our society as a whole. With its great emphasis on psychology and psychiatry, the public has dismissed the idea that suicide is a sin. Having established the link between depression or mental illness and suicide, mental health professionals are generally reluctant to acknowledge suicide or even suicidal thinking as sinful behavior. Even less will they recognize a relation between suicide and one's sinful nature.

A second trend, which perpetuates an ignorance concerning suicide, is evident in the church. Grave misjudgments persist regarding a Christian whose life ends tragically by suicide. Ministers have not addressed adequately *the paradox concerning a Christian's suicide.* To put it in plain terms: "Every Christian knows that killing yourself is a dreadful sin. Yet this person whom we all esteemed as a believer took his own life." And so, in as much as the church has failed to resolve the paradox of a Christian's suicide, the stigma surrounding suicide continues to plague grieving survivors. The question of whether he may have died a Christian remains unanswered. Even if the pastor and family suspect that he did die a believer, they are not permitted to express their belief in any official sort of way.

If the church is to make sufficient strides in removing today's stigma surrounding suicide, it must be the pastor first who aids in the process. When talking about suicide, we must look at the matter from a theological point of view and stress two points: First, our sinful nature is such that Christians like others may inherit a predisposition for depression and hopelessness. Second, while we don't blame suicide exclusively on one's genes—suicide is a sin—neither do we overlook God's unconditional love for sinners. We can trust in God's grace to save even those who commit suicide. Of course we have a long way to go before the church benefits from this teaching. At this time, it is unfortunately the pastors in the church, more than anyone else, who are responsible for suicide's flourishing stigma. Christians have not been educated sufficiently regarding the consequences of having a sinful nature and how Christians too may experience suicidal thinking. Pastors have not taught people concerning the relationship between God's grace and Christian faith, how God sustains faith through his Word and sacraments. Rather than turning to Scripture as a way of resolving suicide's paradox, pastors have relied on human reason. It is assumed that faith cannot survive the horrendous symptoms of depression and absolute hopelessness. It is imagined that faith cannot justify the sinner in the case of suicide.

For the survivors, a major part of grieving is dealing with suicide's stigma. Accordingly, it is the task of the pastor to demonstrate why the persisting stigma associated with suicide has no basis. It is my explicit desire with the title I have chosen for this book to combat this stigma. The reader may recall what was said in the wake of a suicide that hit close to home, perhaps in the local congregation. The first comments typically center on the immediate circumstances surrounding the suicide. Then comes that predictable observation:

"And she was the church's organist!" or "And he was an elder of the congregation!" or "And he was so active in the church's youth group!" In other words: Of all people in the church who might commit such an offense, *this person,* for whom the congregation had such admiration, was not expected to do such a thing. I might summarize the many remarks stating it thus: "And she was a Christian!" Yes, she lost hope. She did not trust in God's gracious will. She in fact sinned, exercising her own will over against God's will. But by God's grace, his Word did not return to him empty but accomplished what he desired (Isaiah 55:11)! She died a believer in Christ!

This book is especially intended for pastors and church professionals who want to help survivors cope with the stigma associated with suicide. It may also prove beneficial to those seeking nonjudgmental answers to the suicide of a Christian loved one.

Part One

My Story as a Survivor

My Beloved Wife, Jean

If you had been acquainted with my wife, Jean, you would remember her as having an exceptionally happy disposition. She was pleasant, easygoing, and extremely easy to befriend. To know her was to know someone who loved life. This was evident in every sector of life. To enter the same room was to be greeted almost instantly by her musical laugh. At the same time, Jean was a perfectionist in some ways. She would not take on something unless she was confident she could do it and do it well. It was her nature. Never did she obligate herself to a given task unless she was prepared to put her heart and soul into it.

This was most evident in Jean's life as a stay-at-home mom of six. The children and I were her first and only priority, and she served with incredible joy and dedication. When Jean was single, she had served as a parochial school teacher. But after we got married, she wanted nothing more than to be a loving mother to her own children, seeing no need to go back to teaching full-time. In her opinion, we had been blessed with a solid marriage and had a good family life. Some might say Jean took her love and devotion to the children to an extreme. After giving birth the fifth time, Jean decided to homeschool our children. I fought it for a time, but she convinced me that it would be beneficial to the whole family. We would spend more time together as a family as the children spent more time at home. The children, furthermore, would excel in their education. In addition to receiving more one-on-one attention from their teacher, they would learn how to work independently. The children would also develop an interest in an assortment of subjects that might otherwise pass them by. For a couple years it seemed to be the right decision. The children learned the basics and much more. They had lessons in Spanish. History and art classes were combined. Mom proved herself to be quite creative in her lesson plans. But more important, Jean was extremely loving and patient. The children loved their new teacher, and they had a very positive attitude about learning.

During our "down time" as a household, Jean did not slow down to a great extent. Some of my fondest memories of Jean are the times we spent together as a family. She was determined that we find time to be together on a daily basis. So we ate at least two meals each day together. Together we vacationed and went on field trips, together

3

we had devotions, and together we went to church. We then ended each day together, as we had the night before. We tucked the children in for the night, said our prayers, and Jean began singing the children to sleep.

In addition to tending to her many duties as a mother and teacher, Jean assisted for a while in the congregations' music programs. At a couple of the churches where I served as pastor, she volunteered her help with directing the choir and playing the organ. Jean loved music. She first started playing the organ at her home congregation at the age of 14. Later she majored in music and became quite accomplished as a vocal soloist. She had an unquestionable gift in her singing. Members of the family said that she had the voice of an angel.

Jean also took an interest in my life as a pastor. She was the one person with whom I could converse on any given subject. She enjoyed keeping informed on matters pertaining to the congregation as well as to the church body to which we belonged. We had many talks on Lutheran theology and church politics. Had she wanted to, I am sure she could have kept up with most pastors of a different persuasion in debating Christian doctrine. Jean was more than the caregiver of my children. She was more than my confidant and companion. As a loving and devoted wife and mother, she provided meaning and perspective to the lives of our entire family.

A Disease Goes Undercover

Jean's happy and fulfilled life would not last, however. After we had been married about ten years, Jean began to suffer from extreme changes in her mood as well as from delusional thinking. Our lives would change quite drastically. Unsurprisingly, Jean's disease, over time, robbed her of her sunny temperament, her commitment as a musician, and her unyielding vigor as a caring wife and mother. In place of Jean's warmth and cheer, a disease emerged whose single purpose was to unload an ever-escalating gloom from which, once entered, there was no return. In place of our loved one, a stranger appeared, who would introduce herself as "Wretched," "Ashamed," "Paranoid," and "Hopeless." After meeting with a psychiatrist and various counselors, I could finally give her condition a name. Jean was suffering from severe clinical depression.

Under most situations, people who are extremely ill will communicate the fact to a few people they trust to obtain needed encouragement and support. Jean, however, insisted that her disease go "undercover." For a long time Jean would not acknowledge that she was ill. She would not admit that she could no longer operate as that independent mother and wife who was always there for us and able to manage our family affairs. As an undercover agent may conceal his true identity even from his closest family and friends, so Jean kept the world around her in the dark. It is not that she was plotting what she might do to the enemy. She *was* the enemy. And she was bent on keeping the truth hidden for the purpose of protecting those she loved the most. What would people think of us if they knew the despicable truth about our wife and mother?

Jean was also very successful in concealing her condition from me. For several months or even years, I remained oblivious to the fact that she was ill, and dangerously ill at that. Once I did learn, of course, I was not willing to be any more honest about Jean's state than she was. For the longest time, I hid from my congregation the fact that Jean was troubled and had to be hospitalized. This continued even after I admitted her on two different occasions to the psychiatric unit of a community hospital. Other than a few neighbors who learned of Jean's state and a couple ladies whom I trusted would not spread the news, my parishioners did not learn of my secret. I did not even include Jean in the Sunday morning prayers. I never went public until after she had successfully taken her life. I did not want to admit that Jean was ill. How would I explain it to others? What would they say?

During the years of Jean's illness, there was much that I did not *want* to see and there was much that I could not *avoid* seeing. The first symptom of her depression that I became aware of was an abnormal thought pattern: People in the church, friends, and even family were not who they seemed to be. No one was to be trusted; at times not even I. Jean's delusions began to subside when—over the course of some months—she was prescribed a number of different medications. In time her symptoms changed. Paranoia was replaced with overwhelming worry. Regrettably, I soon learned that I would never again talk her out of her irrational conclusions. Jean's intense pessimism had to do primarily with our children. She was convinced that they were not learning essential fundamental skills from her homeschooling. This was sure to cause serious problems for them later in life. Unless her parenting abilities were restored very soon, our children were sure to fail in a big way. She also worried immensely about money issues. What about college? What about retirement? In her opinion, she was a continuous drain on our funds. Therefore, family matters would only worsen over time.

I never offered any credence to Jean's fears. Even if there had been a shred of relevance to her claims, her current health was more important. Unfortunately, no words of mine, not even passages from Scripture, could persuade her not to worry. Jean increasingly focused only on those things over which she had no control and blamed herself for everything that seemed to be out of place in her life. It was horrifying to see her once happy life plummet into an ocean of despair. I was at a loss as to what I should do. I was incapable of convincing my wife that she would someday regain that happy life. As she refused to confide in me about her thoughts, it soon became impossible for me to offer encouragement.

Over time I would observe other signs of Jean's depression. She suffered from a form of sadness that could not be considered normal by any standards. She had lost the joy of living. She was certain that she was of no value to anyone. Of course, were she to offer any basis for what she was feeling, she would have convinced no one. What she perceived was merely what she thought *others* perceived. When I learned something about Jean's depression, all I could think of saying to her is that God did not want her to feel so sad. Perhaps if she did a little more praying and reading from Scripture, God would take her sadness away. But I did not offer such advice since it would have only increased her sadness. In her opinion, nothing could rid her of what she was feeling.

Meanwhile, Jean began to feel deep shame because of what her depression was doing to her. She had difficulty keeping up with her obligations. Some friends and I determined that she should receive a break from her parental duties. Our two youngest daughters would stay with friends. Unfortunately, this only deepened her depression further. It did not matter that the arrangement was only temporary. She saw herself a failure as a mother. I learned in a very short time that severe depression never listens to logic. Jean would not fault her depression for her dim outlook on things. Her bleak view of life was perfectly rational in her opinion. Jean, in fact, would blame herself concerning matters over which she had little or no control, instead of asking others for help. It was always "her fault." She refused to connect to her sickness her inability to fulfill various responsibilities.

When shame is permitted to remain in one's life, it may lead to self-loathing. In time I believe Jean had a hard time distinguishing between her illness and herself. Was it her depression that caused her to sleep so much, withdraw from people, obsess over negatives, and made her generally unpleasant to be around? Or was this simply who she was? When I asked Jean whether she might consider doing some minor housework instead of lying in bed, I remember later regretting it. My proposal merely helped build her case against herself. She would rather sleep the day away than do something constructive as the mother of the house. Even if I argued that she had nothing to feel guilty about and I was fortunate enough to shoot down every charge she filed against herself, there was always something else she could pin on herself. There was always one more damning piece of evidence. I remember Jean telling me, "You wouldn't love me if you knew what I did." Although to this day I am not sure what it was, I have always presumed it was some former delusion she could not let go of—a false memory of sorts. In any case, she had neither the energy nor the courage to tell me about it. It was easier to let "the truth" as she perceived it go untold.

As I came to understand more about severe depression, I determined that it might be best described as unrelenting, excruciating pain. The life that had once brought her happiness and a sense of purpose was gone, never again to be reclaimed. She would never be the mother she wanted to be. Our family was heading toward very difficult times for which she was responsible, and nothing could reroute our destiny. I am convinced these thoughts were on her mind constantly and served to perpetuate her hopeless mood.

As an attempt to elaborate on what was surely unimaginable pain, I might relate an experience of mine. My family of eight was taking a walk on the other side of the lake from our cabin in northern Minnesota. We followed a path that led into the woods. Within just a matter of moments, the native mosquitoes came out in all their fury. We literally were being eaten alive. I will never forget Jean's indifference over the matter. Had I not cried out to the rest of the family, "We're turning back; let's get back to the boat now!" I do not believe Jean would have ever caught on. She was absolutely oblivious to the mosquitoes. What I might have described as unbearable—the thickest, hungriest swarm of mosquitoes I had ever seen—did not compare to the misery Jean was already experiencing.

Uncharted Territory

Until I was forced to deal with Jean's depression and delusional thinking, I was not aware that her family had a history of mental illness. Had I been capable of looking ahead when Jean's depression first peeked its head out, I would never have imagined embarking on

7

such a humbling journey. Looking back to the day of her suicide, it is obvious that I did not comprehend the ramifications of her act.

Immediately following the terrorist attack on September 11, 2001, New York City mayor Rudolph Giuliani was evaluating the situation with the chief of the New York City fire department. The mayor made a profound remark as they looked up together and saw a body falling from one of the twin towers. "We've entered uncharted territory," he said, referring to the United States and some obvious adjustments our nation would have to make. If you know a person suffering heartache because of a recent suicide in the family, that person may feel that he and his family have entered uncharted territory. The challenge they must now confront is one for which they have not been prepared. A life-altering event has thrust itself upon them. However, they neither signed up for this nor consented to it. After the dust has settled, in fact, the only thing they can manage to do is ask a number of disturbing questions: How did this happen to my loved one? What will people think? Is there something I could have done to prevent his death? Is there something someone else could have done? How will I go on?

I asked these questions for some time, beginning that day when my life was forever altered. It was Jean's first morning home following her second hospital stay. I was working in my office, which was connected to the church parsonage. Suddenly I sensed that something in the house was not right. It was too quiet. Wasting no time, I searched our home from top to bottom and found Jean in an isolated room of the basement. She was lying unconscious in a fetal position with a plastic bag covering her head.

Much of what followed in the next several hours is a blur to this day. I remember phoning the operator instead of 9-1-1. I remember the paramedics in my house who promptly checked for a pulse. I remember the ambulance ride. And I remember—as I sat somewhere adjacent to the emergency room—my agonizing wait for some word on Jean's condition. Could they help her? Would I lose her? Would she succeed in her second attempt to end her life? What if she lived? Would she be in a coma? It took one brief instant for a nurse in the next room with a seemingly cavalier remark to answer most of the questions rushing through my head. If I remember her words correctly, she said, "There's too much brain damage; I don't think she's going to regain consciousness." Had that nurse known that I was listening, she might have restricted her comment to those in the same room where they worked in futile fashion to revive my wife. Then again, I do not think the words would have been any easier to accept had they been spoken to me directly. There was nothing anyone could have uttered right then to make the ensuing hours or days or months any easier. Jean died 36 hours later because of prolonged oxygen deficiency to the brain.

In my efforts to absorb what had just happened, I immediately realized something. I did not have the luxury of retreating into my own little world. I had obligations. Despite my personal trauma, I had to phone my parents. But how was I to tell them? Surely they would be devastated by the news. This was just the beginning of my overwhelming questions. What would I say to my children? How would I manage as a father of six between the ages of 14 months and 12 years? How could I pastor a congregation of more than five hundred members? No one had an answer. Furthermore, there was one more question that proved more troubling than the rest. And unlike the other questions, this final one would *not* remain unanswered. In fact, in my mind it had been answered with absolute finality. Whose fault was it and why? What might I have done to prevent this catastrophe?

The Question About Her Death

Despite how busy my children and congregation kept me the year Jean died, the question concerning blame continued to torment me. Part of the problem, as the weeks and months passed, was that I became mindful of another question. It was *the* question concerning Jean's death. People were bound to ask me how my wife died. How was I to let myself off the hook when no one was more familiar with Jean's troubles than I? Why should I *not* feel guilty about her death when I was the first person in a position to prevent this tragedy? In the end, there was no way to avoid the question, short of avoiding people who might be inclined to ask it.

Then again, whether a loved one dies by suicide or some other means is to a certain extent immaterial, since the question concerning death is unavoidable. People will always ask "How did he die?" "How did she die?" The question, after all, expresses concern. People want to be supportive. Perhaps their father or mother died the same way. Knowing something of your latest burden, they can console you. However, most acquaintances you speak to do not expect to hear you say, "She committed suicide." That manner of death is one that is forbidden in people's minds. Much needed comfort and support, hence, is often lacking. When I tell people that Jean took her life, they typically do not know what to say. The most frequent response is "Oh, I'm sorry!" as if to say "Oh, that's horrible! How do I comfort you now?!"

Today I do have an easier time talking about Jean's death than I did in the beginning. However, when people ask me how Jean died, it is not my custom in every case to answer their question with a brief one-sentence reply: "She committed suicide." More typically, I will explain that she was suffering from depression and died by suicide. If they then want to visit with me about her illness, I am very happy to oblige.

I became aware that Jean was suffering mentally shortly before she became pregnant with our sixth child. Some months later she was diagnosed as having clinical depression. Over the course of time, she gave up various activities such as homeschooling the four older children, directing the church choir, and volunteering for various projects at church and school. Although I did not consider the possibility until more recently, Jean probably suffered from various symptoms of depression for a number of years. And I am sure she suffered more than once under postpartum depression.

Why did I not pick up on the fact that she was sick? Perhaps it had something to do with my disposition. I would not describe myself as a natural caregiver. I am fairly empathetic by nature, but I am also a fairly unassuming individual. Sometimes I find it a little too easy, in fact, to let others assume the role of taking charge. I believe that was the case when I was married to Jean. I was not used to making decisions for Jean without her consent. Making matters worse, she neglected to let me know how bad things were getting. It should have been obvious to me that Jean needed to be hospitalized. Standing on my own, however, I was not willing to make the call. The decision came upon the advice of her psychiatrist. He asked Jean whether she had had any suicidal thoughts. I was astonished to hear from my wife of nearly 13 years that she had thoughts of killing herself. That day I learned a bit more about the illness of major depression and the reluctance of those suffering under this disease to share their thoughts. Jean might have been in the deepest anguish imaginable, while those closest to her hadn't the slightest clue. It did not matter as far as she was concerned. Telling us what she was going through would serve no purpose.

In the months that followed, Jean's mental state continued to erode despite the efforts of her psychiatrist and various psychologists and counselors. She was hospitalized on two occasions after admitting that she was suicidal. Jean, my wife of 13 years, died in September

1994, after her second attempt to take her life. She was 41 years old and left behind her husband and six children, ranging in age between 1 year and 12.

Dealing With the Stigma

Prompted by ignorance

It is normal as a survivor to grieve when you lose a loved one. You have been separated from someone to whom you have grown close and shared many things through the years. A suicide survivor has the further burden of dealing with a stigma that tends to malign whomever it touches. Prompted by ignorance, the stigma arrives unannounced and demands an answer to one particular question: What kind of person would choose suicide? It does not matter who attempts to answer the question. No room is allowed for understanding. The question merely invites criticism and promotes putting the worse construction on things. Webster's *Living Dictionary* defines the word *stigma:* "Any mark of infamy; a blemish or stain, as on one's character; a brand of disgrace attached to a person."[1] Within a given context, this may include the belief that one has cause to make a judgment without an understanding of the facts. The result is that a person is unjustly labeled. Others who are often stigmatized are the mentally ill, the disabled, people of various minority groups, and those who divorce. The obvious difference with a suicide is that the labeled person has no voice. Having died, he cannot address those judging him.

The stigma of suicide by nature is also very subtle. An acquaintance may say to one of the survivors, "Oh, you poor thing!" But what do those words mean? Do they reflect empathy for their loss, or do the words have something to say about the regrettable nature of how their loved one died? The survivor must decide for himself. In another situation, a friend or loved one might not say anything that could be taken the wrong way but may choose instead to pity those who are left behind. Pity, however, simply results in one being manipulated by the stigma. Even caring gestures based on pity in the end serve as little more than a nonverbal question that goes something like this: "How do you deal with this death, knowing what you do?"

Suicide's stigma, to be sure, is not always kept discreet. It is often verbalized. And this permits the stigma to perpetuate. Generalizations are made regarding those who take their own lives. At one time you may have uttered the words yourself: "He was crazy!" Or "The family had issues!" Or if the suicide was an acquaintance, you may have remarked: "I never would have imagined he was the type!"

Following Jean's suicide, I soon began torturing myself over people's presumed responses. What were family and friends going to think? Jean was so dedicated, so caring. But no one would be thinking much about that now. They would be asking how she could do such a thing. How could she be so selfish? I do not believe it was so much what I actually heard, as it was what I imagined people were saying: "How come she wasn't thinking about her children, her husband, her family?" "What kind of Christian would choose suicide?" "Isn't depression something we must learn to simply live with?" "So, she was depressed!" "Don't we all get sick?" "Why couldn't she beat it? Had she a stronger faith, she would not have remained in her state of depression." "If she had only taken a closer look at the many blessings she had received from her Lord, she would not have ended her life so tragically."

I do recall some specific words relating to Jean's depression that had been related to my mother before Jean's death. A friend had suggested that Jean was feeling sorry for herself and simply needed to get over her mood. Then she saw Jean. Perhaps it was the sunken eyes. Or it was the expression of utter emptiness, the face of despair. She later commented to my mother that she understood.

Perpetuated by fear

While suicide's stigma is created by ignorance, it is just as true to say that it is perpetuated by fear. To put it as simply as I can, people are afraid that they or their loved ones could be susceptible to the same fate. Their reaction therefore is a type of defense mechanism. People want to know: "This couldn't happen to me." When a person is faced with the unknown, it is natural to feel vulnerable. But how can you be confident that you will be spared what has proved so devastating for someone else? The easiest way of overcoming your fear is by taking the focus off you and laying blame somewhere else. The stigma of suicide gives you permission to do this. Unfortunate conclusions are drawn about the individual and his family. Thoughts take on a presumptuous air: "How awful! I wonder what happened to So-and-so. Thank God suicide could never torment our household!" I have always wondered what prompted some neighborhood children to ring our doorbell one day shortly after Jean's suicide. They lived a couple houses away and like my children had a father who was a minister. It was not the first time they stopped by, but it was apparent this one day that their intention was not to play. They had something else on their minds, something to share: "We heard your mom killed herself by putting a bag over head!" they related, as if to say, "Our mommy would never do something like that!"

Many words said in innocence can be quite hurtful. Other words, intended to offer support, are just as unfortunate. There was the long-time friend of my mother who, in a feeble attempt to sound under-standing, told her, "You don't have to worry about my husband and me! We won't tell anyone!" This woman may have been naïve regard-ing how her comments would affect my mother, but perhaps she understood something about human nature. Inasmuch as no one is immune to suicide, it scares people. Fear gives way to judgment with respect to the one who took his life as well as his family. The judg-ment is then verbalized to others, perhaps a number of others. And the news spreads at an unbelievable rate.

Every survivor is affected

It is not simply those looking from the outside in who are affected by suicide's stigma. Members of the immediate family are too, although they may react to the suicide in a far different manner. Instead of issu-ing their judgments, they retreat into a defense mode and say an assortment of things in order to protect the reputation of the suicide and his family. Or perhaps they just do not know what to say. What comes to mind is a pastoral conference I attended shortly after my wife died. A former classmate of mine asked my father and me what hap-pened to Jean. My father was quicker in issuing a response than I. He told the fellow pastor. "She had depression, and she just died!" He could not bring himself to say the word *suicide* in front of me and this other pastor whom we both respected. Presumably, I would be too humiliated by our acknowledgment of the event. My father was not only the president of the seminary my classmate and I had attended, he was considered by many to be the greatest theologian of our church body. With a little effort, he could have given a very solid explanation as to why suicide's stigma had no scriptural basis. But at this particu-lar moment, he was more concerned about my feelings than with offer-ing this gentleman a theological perspective on the subject. To this day I love and respect my father for what he attempted to do in front of this pastor. The fact that he said what he did and I did not correct him has helped me understand something. It does not matter who you are. If you lose a loved one to suicide, you will be affected by the stigma.

The stigma of suicide also affected my talks with my children. At the time Jean died, I told my children that their mother's heart had simply stopped. I realized my explanation was simply a delaying tactic. I was not ready to tell them the painful truth, and they were not ready to hear it. It is not that I was afraid of traumatizing them or something to that effect. Most of my children were quite young and would not have comprehended what death was, much less the act of suicide. And yet I was afraid of what they would say someday if asked by a friend or acquaintance how their first mom died. How would people react to my children's words when they mentioned their mother's suicide? The last thing I wanted for them was to feel shame when talking about Jean's death. Young people, like those kids next door, can especially be very blunt with their words, whether knowingly or unknowingly.

Doctrinal in nature

Much of the stigma that persists today is of a religious or doctrinal nature. It is assumed that the suicide must have been not only deranged but also evil. People speculate: "He was copping out on life and giving up on God. Those who commit suicide are cowards, thinking only of themselves. If only he had been more trusting!" Such talk, mind you, is one little step from deeming that the suicide was not a believer or that he did not have the Christian base required to deal with his difficulties.

Christian ministers too have been affected by the stigma. Although it may not come out in a funeral sermon, preachers often avoid addressing the issue. They do not want to alienate the family, implying that their loved one may have lost the final battle. Unfortunately, the lack of leadership on this issue has only worsened suicide's stigma. If ministers are comfortable remaining uninformed about Christians who commit suicide, we can be sure many others in the church are too. It takes less work, to be sure, to remain ignorant than it does to develop an understanding of what triggers suicide.

It is my experience that some of the worst judgers may be those who have personally experienced some depression. The problem for some is that they really do not know what clinical depression is, having suffered from a less severe form of depression. Or if they were severely depressed at one point and perhaps suicidal, they attribute their recovery in part to their Christian faith.

We may spend little time discussing the subject of suicide before we agree that suicide is sinful. It is never a good choice no matter who you are. This does not excuse us, however, from educating ourselves about depression, mental illness, and other factors that heighten a sense of hopelessness. The questions I wish to answer in the chapters that follow are straightforward. What is behind the stigma that is associated with suicide? In addition, what might you and I say within the church of Christ to help rid our culture of this stigma? Suicide's stigma will thrive, I am afraid, as long as people in the church maintain that suicide is an unforgivable sin or that no one with true faith could bring himself to commit suicide.

Suicide's Paradox

Suicide's stigma persists today because people have been exposed to an assortment of paradoxes having to do with suicide and they do not know how to respond to the paradoxes or resolve them. A paradox can be defined as a statement that, although true, is seemingly self-contradicting. I may cite one example from Scripture. God is just, threatening eternal condemnation to those who fail to do everything written in the Book of the Law (Galatians 3:10). Yet God is gracious, desiring to save all people (1 Timothy 2:3,4). To someone who has not been instructed in the Christian faith, these two statements seem to contradict each other. The paradox is resolved, however, when it is explained that we observe both the judgment of God and the grace of God in the suffering and death of Jesus Christ. Jesus was condemned so that sinners might *not* be. Thus, you and I are saved by faith in Christ. In the wake of a suicide, we observe any one of a number of paradoxes. It may be said that a Christian trusts in God and in his many blessings, yet this Christian despaired and gave up on those same blessings. A stigma forms when people are confronted with an apparent contradiction and the contradiction is not resolved, at least not in an adequate way. One may deduce, for example, that to despair or lose hope that God will again bless you in this life is to give up on God's grace, or that the Christian who despairs and takes his life has surely lost his faith. This obviously puts the suicide in a very bad light. And so the stigma linked with suicide persists. The stigma will thrive, in fact, so long as attempts to resolve the seeming contradictions are based on something other than the facts and the truth of Scripture.

It is a task many, regrettably, will avoid: making an effort to resolve the paradox and answer why a particular Christian has *really* chosen suicide. If you have ministered to a family affected by a suicide, you may have chosen to ignore the stigma. Skirting the issue, perhaps you told the grieving there are certain things in this life that we cannot understand. Many pastors have determined, I'm sure, that the mourning family will find it easier to simply endure the stigma

15

associated with suicide and live with it the best they can. If your intent is *not* to respond to suicide's stigma in this way, I commend you. Furthermore, my objective is to offer you an invaluable alternative. Let us not acquiesce to the stigma, as this will merely inhibit survivors from working through their grief. Let us instead challenge the misconceptions and unfair judgments about Christians who take their own lives. We can do so, I believe, only by addressing the paradoxes with which we are confronted following a Christian's suicide.

Not helping matters, meanwhile, are the countless people outside of the family who have assigned to themselves the task of resolving this apparent paradox. They have been informed of this Christian who apparently self-destructed. In some cases they may know this person. What happened? Did he lose his faith? If so, what would account for this? And if he did not lose his faith in Christ, how could he carry out such a dreadful act? Unfortunately, few such people will truly succeed in resolving the paradox. They may make a case for attaching blame to particular family members and others who presumably played an adverse role in the life of the suicide prior to his death. But they do not truly answer the question of why a Christian would commit suicide, unless of course he was not really a Christian at all—not at the moment he took his life anyway.

This explains another whole dimension of survivor guilt, one that grieving Christians are convinced will forever torment them. They speculate whether—despite the fact that it was the time God appointed for their husband or wife, child or parent, brother or sister to go home—their loved one possibly may *not* have gone home to heaven. They are afraid they should have given him stronger warnings. They should have told him that what he was contemplating was sinful. They should have informed him that the mere thought of taking his life could compromise his faith. When it comes to survivor guilt, it may make little difference in one sense whether our loved one committed suicide or died by some other means. Regardless of death's cause, survivors will frequently ask themselves whether they are responsible, whether there was not something more they could have done. With respect to the suicide survivor, however, family and friends may torture themselves over the questions: Was he saved? If not, am I to blame if this family member or friend is spending eternity in hell? Many suicide survivors feel that the only way they can come to accept the death of their loved one is if they are confident this child or spouse or parent, etc., was a Christian and remained in the faith despite his suicide.

It is precisely this confidence you may offer parishioners who mourn following the suicide of a loved one. Talk about their family member who has died. Talk then about what it means to be a Christian. Explain that if a Christian is one who trusts in Christ alone and his redeeming work, we may agree that a Christian suicide is an apparent contradiction. Such a tragedy should not occur. Paradoxes exist, however, in a world where God is gracious to sinners, where God is "alive and well" but so is sin and its effects. I have come to appreciate immensely what God's Word has taught me with respect to the tragedy of a suicide as it relates to God's care and Christ's forgiveness. Nothing in life happens by chance. Just as it was God's choice to have his Son die for every one of Jean's sins, so it was according to his gracious will to deliver my wife from this vale of tears at the precise time that she died.

Understanding Versus Justification

Some will maintain, I am sure, that this book should not have been written. "To presume and to declare that a person can commit suicide at a time when he has faith is to let him off the hook" the thinking goes. I do not believe this is the case. Understanding an issue as important as the suicide of a Christian is not the same thing as justification. At the same time, this book is not written to offer the depressed and hopeless a motive for considering suicide. If you are suicidal, this book will offer no strategy for making a final exit to a better existence. My charge to you is to talk with those you love about what you perceive is wrong with your life and seek immediate help. There is nothing degrading about obtaining assistance from someone who has been trained to offer you solutions to a current health crisis.

For you who are not suicidal but would simply like to make sense out of what seems nonsensical, I intend to demonstrate that suicide does not necessarily coincide with unbelief. The majority of those who commit suicide—like my wife, Jean—suffer under major depression or an overwhelming sense of hopelessness. It makes little difference whether the individual was struggling because of a mood disorder, because of enormous stress in life, or because he experienced a recent major change in his life. In almost every case, the suicide chooses death after perceiving that there is no end to his troubles.

Many people fail to understand this about suicide. Serving as a fitting example may be a pastor who stopped by moments after Jean arrived at the hospital. After finding me, he immediately asked,

"Why would she do this? She was a mother of six beautiful children! She had so much to live for!" Looking back, I am sure this was his way of expressing empathy. However, it was very evident to me that he did not understand the first thing about severe clinical depression. The Christian survivor is best consoled in his grief when he is reassured that this loved one who preceded him in death was a fellow believer. A problem exists when those who wish to comfort the survivor have doubts about this person who took his life. Then the burden of proof is placed on the grieving person who still seeks words of support.

My aim in the following chapters is to provide a strategy for pastors and Christian educators and counselors who offer hope to suicide survivors. Those who struggle to make sense out of their crushing loss will ask how someone they knew as a Christian could die by suicide. Many of the questions they ask in their grief, unfortunately, never get answered. I consider myself fortunate to have worked through the questions over which I once agonized. With the aid of Scripture and various other sources, it is my hope to offer you help with what to say to the grieving who seek both to understand and to cope with suicide's stigma.

In part two, I will show how the church has often failed in its efforts to resolve the paradoxes. With its false teachings on suicide and faith, the church continues to deprive those who grieve of the comfort of the gospel. In parts two and three, I intend to resolve the paradoxes associated with a believer's suicide, thereby aiding in the effort to overcome suicide's stigma. I will do so by presenting a thorough biblical explanation first of faith, then of sin and grace and how the three pertain to the depressed and hopeless. Assisting in this process will be several case studies, including some personal comments pertaining to my wife's suicide. In part four, you will receive specific suggestions as to what you might say to the grieving family member who is inclined to blame everyone under the sun— himself, the suicide, the immediate family, even God. So that my comments may prove more user friendly, I have written them in the second person, as though I am speaking directly to the one who is grieving. Part five: "Gospel Relief for the Hopeless" is written for church leaders who seek to minister to and obtain help for those experiencing hopelessness but who often have misconceptions on how to do so.

If you are not a suicide survivor, please be mindful that you can be most supportive by not drawing immediate conclusions as to why this person made such a bad and tragic decision. Rather than seeking grounds for judging, please resolve to be encouraging with your words. Tell the surviving families how Scripture offers comfort regarding the salvation of known believers. Irrespective of the hurtful choices God's people make when affected by depression and mental illness, God still saves by grace. In every case, he promises to those whom he has kept in the faith, the glories of heaven with our gracious and ever-living Savior.

Notes

[1]Noah Webster, *The Living Webster Encyclopedic Dictionary of the English Language* (Chicago: The English Language Institute of America, 1975), p. 960.

Part Two

The Church's Case Against the Suicide

There is a predominant notion that has been expressed over the years concerning a Christian who commits suicide: we cannot know anything for sure regarding his destiny. Even if we knew this person as a believer, it would be presumptuous at the time of his death to find comfort in God's grace and the forgiveness of sins. Over the years I have heard several pastors express uncertainty with regard to how to deal with a suicide in their parishes. They have questioned whether we can truly know if a given suicide was a believer at the time he died. Specifically, I have heard it said, "We must leave the matter to the gracious judgment of our Lord. We cannot really know what was in his heart."

A stigma exists when a majority is willing to remain silent or uninformed about a label that is unfairly fastened to a particular people. The same stigma becomes more severe when a respected sector of the population approves of the stigma. This is true of the church with respect to suicide's stigma. If it were not for a large percentage of clergy who remain uneducated concerning depression and suicide, I do not believe the stigma surrounding suicide would amount to much. But the stigma persists. And it dates back over a span of many years.

Chapter 1

POSTHUMOUS JUDGMENTS OF
YESTERDAY AND TODAY

 Every believer knows full well that suicide is a dreadful sin. Still, this Christian proceeded to take his own life.

The church historically has done a better job of addressing the *sin* of suicide than it has of acknowledging in any consistent sort of way that a given suicide was a *Christian*. This has made it next to impossible to resolve satisfactorily the paradox of a Christian's suicide. Instead of offering a suitable answer as to why Christians commit suicide, church leaders have, in fact, contributed to the stigma of suicide. Pastors, to a large extent, have handled the issue of suicide in one of two ways. They have asserted that suicide is the one sin no one with faith can possibly commit, or they have kept it a mystery as to whether the church may acknowledge the deceased as having been a believer.

The Church Responds to an Epidemic

How did the early church address the problem of suicide?

For most contemporary Western Christians, it is nearly impossible to imagine one's struggle to stay alive in a society dedicated to wiping out the gospel. That was the situation for the earliest Christians. To be branded a Christian meant facing horrifying and humiliating forms of execution. As a result, many Christians turned to suicide as an alternative. In time, believers even came to justify their self-killing. Suicide was not merely a means of escaping torment. It was a mode of confessing the faith. You would be remembered as a martyr, a most attractive option over an otherwise horrible and demeaning end.

Some Christians were convinced it was merely a matter of time before they were tracked down and fed to the lions. So they met their executioners halfway. They chose to profess their faith in public, where they were immediately discovered and apprehended by the authorities. Proponents would reference words spoken by Christ, who promoted self-sacrifice among his disciples. They might shout, for example, "Greater love has no one than this, that he lay down his life for his friends" (John 15:13) or "Whoever wants to save his life will lose it, but whoever loses his life for me will find it" (Matthew 16:25) just before they jumped from a bridge into a raging river.

As the threat increased and also the likelihood that they would die, the distinction between dying by another's hand and one's own hand became less relevant. That made suicide a lot easier. They would go down in history as those who died for the faith. Many eventually regarded martyrdom as a second baptism, a "baptism by blood." Tailored after the bloody death of Christ, Christians were sprinkled with the baptism of blood. It was not uncommon, in fact, for Christian converts to slay themselves immediately after they were baptized. By killing themselves before they succumbed to temptation, they were assured of eternal salvation since they died in a state of grace.[1] Being martyred very logically had become the quickest ticket to heaven.

By the fourth century, suicide among Christians had become an epidemic. For the welfare of believers, it was imperative that the church become more outspoken on the matter. They should address how suicide was in direct opposition to the commandment "You shall not murder." A distinction should be made between suicide and martyrdom. It was the church father Augustine who in time would successfully impose his view about suicide on the church. What he declared in his work *The City of God* would eventually become the official position of the Roman church.

> But this we affirm, this we maintain, this we every way pronounce to be right, that no man ought to inflict on himself voluntary death, for *this is to escape the ills of time by plunging into those of eternity;* . . . that no man should put an end to this life to obtain that better life we look for after death, *for those who die by their own hand have no better life after death.*[2]

Augustine's position continued through the Middle Ages and would become the established doctrine of the church. The sin of suicide was deemed unforgivable. The only exception was if it could be established that the suicide was "out of his mind."

In the years to follow, it was not open for debate whether and how the deceased were judged. Suicide was classified as a mortal sin suggested by the devil.[3] By the twelfth century, it had become canon law that a suicide be refused a Christian burial.[4] Heirs were also punished, as their assets and household belongings were confiscated by the local government.

Superstition's Duel With Satan

A short time before Jean ended her life, I am quite sure she believed she was under assault. She never commented on specifics with me, but I sensed that her misguided conscience had a lock on her thoughts rather than the assurances of Scripture. She also may have believed Satan had a voice in the matter. I recall my father commenting on a chapter he had just completed writing on demon possession. He explained how the devil uses his power not only to possess unbelievers, but in some instances to torment believers. Jean became extremely agitated by my father's words, as though my father was clearly speaking about her.

Is it possible she was possessed?

The opinion that suicide be linked to Satan was soon unanimous. The devil had lured people to end their own lives, persuading them they could no longer rely on God's mercy and that damnation was certain. The church had judged that suicide be recognized as the one sin for which one automatically was excluded from God's grace. Posthumous judgments in the church became a matter of both doctrine and practice. As one branded "unbeliever," the suicide was buried in that part of the cemetery reserved for the excommunicated, the unbaptized, and others who were deprived of eternal salvation.

The judgments, moreover, did not end with edicts from the local parish condemning the soul to hell. Fear and superstition demanded that the corpse itself be punished. If the people were not issued a stern warning about what happened to suicides, Satan would surely claim further victims. In many cases stakes were driven through the body of the suicide. This would serve not only in deterring the possessed body from resurrecting, but also to keep it from disturbing the living. It prevented evil from spreading. In addition, the bodies of suicides were often carried facedown or headfirst to the burial. This too was done in order to frustrate the spirit, discouraging it from finding its way back to survivors.[5] Other penalties designed to mislead the spirit involved burying the body at a crossroads or severing the hands and head and burying them apart from the body. One law of medieval France demanded that the body of a suicide be removed from the house through an opening dug under the threshold, thrown into the

25

river, and nailed up in a barrel bearing a sign commanding that it be left to drift. The accursed body would thus be borne far away, without polluting the local river water.[6]

The penalties against suicide served one simple purpose: isolate the corpse from the surviving believers, protecting the Christian community from demon possession. Originating in the early Middle Ages, they became matters of common law by the thirteenth century. As late as the eighteenth century, the bodies of suicides were denied burial in consecrated ground, were required to be buried by night, and underwent trials. In the end, the corpse was sentenced to be beaten with chains and then was burned.

Today demon possession is often associated with superstition. It is no longer a custom of the church to establish a connection between those who die by suicide and people who are assaulted by a demon. Perhaps we have reached a consensus in the church today. It shall never be said of the devil that he "made me do it!" Possession denotes total ownership, and this cannot hold true for the Christian who is owned by Christ. Through Baptism we have received the gift of the Holy Spirit (Acts 2:38) and have put on Christ (Galatians 3:27). The result is, whether we live or die, we belong to the Lord (Romans 14:8). No one, especially the devil, can lay claim to our souls or our bodies.

Satan may not exercise ownership over the Christian and thus possess him. There is another category, though, which often goes unmentioned and of which we can cite examples both from Scripture and today's situation. We may call it "demon affliction." During Jesus' ministry, our Lord encountered many people who were afflicted with physical handicaps or deficiencies. In Matthew a demonized man who is blind and mute is brought to Jesus (Matthew 12:22). In St. Luke's gospel, Jesus is teaching in a synagogue and meets a woman who had been crippled by a spirit for 18 years (Luke 13:11). St. Paul, because of his surpassingly great revelations, was given a thorn in his flesh, a messenger of Satan, to "torment" him (2 Corinthians 12:7). And then there is Job, who is blameless and upright but is "afflicted" by Satan (Job 2:7) with unbearable sores from head to foot. We may make a case for demon affliction in today's world. Satan finds an ally in certain illnesses with their unyielding assaults on a person's sense of well-being. He does not enter the Christian and manipulate his every movement as when he possesses an unbeliever. He assaults the Christian from the outside with the purpose of getting him to question his Lord's boundless mercy. The depressed individual may be the devil's favorite target. The believer hears the accusations of his disease, "You're lazy, unproductive, a burden to those around you! You're nothing but a failure, unworthy of God's love!" and the devil is more than happy to record the allegations, playing them over and over again in the head of the accused. Anything that keeps this person from hearing words concerning Christ's forgiveness is a good thing as far as Satan is concerned.

Then again, in one sense we *all* suffer affliction under Satan. Behind the scenes, in ways that remain unidentified, Satan assaults mankind. He attacks not just you and me, but on a much larger scale he is responsible for aggressive offensives against societies of the world, the church, and even nature. In evil and destructive ways, he haunts people and corrupts creation. Everyone professing the Christian faith in effect can expect to come under the devil's vicious, relentless attacks. The apostle warns, "Our struggle is not against flesh and blood, but against the rulers, against the authorities, against the powers of this dark world and against the spiritual forces of evil in the heavenly realms" (Ephesians 6:12).

All of us experience the devil's assaults. However, the vast majority of the Christian population does not respond by resorting to suicide. Thus, in the final analysis, there is no testimony from Scripture dealing with demon activity that allows us to assert that people who take their own lives do so because they gave in to the pressure of Satan and abandoned "the good fight" (2 Timothy 4:7).

The Modern Course of Action

Should today's pastors conduct a funeral for a parishioner who commits suicide?

At the time of my wife's funeral, I may have had an advantage over other suicide survivors. I would set the tone at the time of the service. My father would offer some personal comments before the service began. My brother would preach the sermon. Another brother would serve as the liturgist. Because I was the pastor of the church, there was never any question about where or whether the service would be held. My wife was a Christian. No one would go home that day without receiving every assurance that she was in heaven.

You and I may agree. No one is better qualified in defining what a Christian is than one active in the church's ministry. Furthermore, no one will be less likely to draw a wrong conclusion about a given Christian, asserting that he has lost his faith. It is something we might even assume. Today's pastors and theologians will be most effective in helping resolve the great paradox of a Christian's suicide and to

27

eliminate the stigma that accompanies it. Regrettably, the church, as in former days, has often done more to foster a spirit of judgment than to minister to the depressed and despairing. This is due largely to the words we have spoken to parishioners following the suicide of someone in the congregation. Although quite thorough in our explanation of why suicide is a sin, we have failed to address why sinners *choose* suicide. To the extent that we have failed to talk about God's grace for the foulest of sins, we have advocated an environment in the church today in which suicide's stigma may prosper.

You may ask how the average pastor will respond when he first learns that a member has committed suicide. Does he ask how he will comfort the survivors? Or is the question whether a Christian burial may be offered or not? Admittedly, our seminary education has not always proved very helpful in this area. Seminary textbooks have suggested that a Christian pastor may officiate *only* at such funerals where it is evident that the member who took his own life cannot be held responsible for having done so, as in cases of insanity or high fevers. However, you should never officiate at the funeral of a suicide who *intentionally* took his own life.[7] But how do you determine such a thing? Presumably you must rely on the professional judgment of someone who may know little or nothing about Christian faith in order to make a decision about whether he will have a Christian funeral. In some congregations, funeral rites are withheld from the suicide unless the family acquires a letter from the family physician, stating that the deceased was under treatment for a psychotic or emotional disorder.[8] So the suicide is presumed guilty of unbelief until proved insane.

Naturally, it would not be extremely practical for you to try and determine whether a suicide is mentally ill before you commit to holding a service. Current tradition dictates a more gentle method of expressing judgment against suicide. It may be customary in your congregation for the service to be held in the funeral home rather than the church. Funerals in the sanctuary are reserved for those perceived to be members in good standing. Or if it is held in the church, perhaps you have felt a duty to spend some time preaching about the sin of suicide. You must be discreet in what you say about this person who professed the Christian faith. If you assure the family that this loved one is in heaven with his Savior and say nothing about his suicide, you might inadvertently encourage someone else to contemplate taking his life. Presumably, you have a choice. Condemn the sin of suicide, or say nothing about suicide and assert nothing about this Christian's entrance into heaven.

Certainly the church has the responsibility to interpret Scripture in a trustworthy manner. With little study of God's Word, we conclude that suicide is sinful. It is a form of murder. The church, however, may not judge, in any given case, whether a professing believer, having died by suicide, died an unbeliever. It is not the crime that determines what is in the heart. It is the heart that determines the crime. "Out of the *heart* come evil thoughts, murder, adultery, sexual immorality, theft, false testimony, slander" (Matthew 15:19). Can the same heart that possesses faith in the only Savior also entertain evil thoughts and commit suicide? Unfortunately, yes. You ought never deny a Christian funeral to a member who dies by suicide or issue other judgments, unless perhaps you have confirmed the fact that this person has verbally denied the faith. Even in such circumstances, however, I would be very cautious. People suffering from serious depression or schizophrenia have been known to make very bizarre claims, insisting that God despises them and they are going to hell. Observers may suggest that they are denying the most basic truths of the Christian faith. The facts indicate they are severely delusional. For this reason, if you are ever tempted to judge that a fellow believer has abandoned the faith based on his suicide, my advice to you is quite simple. Ask yourself some simple questions. Was the suicide a member in good standing of your congregation? Was he baptized? Apart from any recent peculiar behavior on his part, did his family and closest friends know him to be a Christian?

If a person confessed the Christian faith, there should be no question as to whether we offer a Christian burial. Personally, I find it quite interesting, significant to be sure, that David blessed those who buried Saul. You will remember that Saul fell on his own sword when his three sons died in battle against the Philistines and Saul himself was critically wounded. When David was informed about those who buried Saul, he relayed a message to the men responsible for his burial: "The LORD bless you for showing this kindness to Saul your master by burying him" (2 Samuel 2:5). David does not see Saul's unfortunate death as an opportunity to subject the former king's corpse and reputation to shame. Instead, he commends and blesses those who offer him a proper burial (1 Samuel 31:11-13). It is not evident to me that Saul was a believer. Neither is it my purpose to suggest that pastors today perform funerals for those who denied the faith. However, if King David encouraged a proper burial for suicides, it certainly behooves us as Christian pastors today to do the same. If there is any doubt about whether a member was a believer at the

29

time of his suicide, we ought to hold a funeral. Err on the side of grace. And let us have it in the church where it's done for any other member in good standing, not in a funeral home, as has often been the customary action of judgment.

Until now, perhaps you have dealt with the suicide issue hypothetically. Perhaps you have little trouble agreeing with me that a Christian funeral is supposed to be a service for the survivors. The primary purpose for holding a funeral is to comfort the grieving believer. It is not to make a statement about the deceased's transgression. In addition, to hold the same kind of funeral for a suicide as you do for others is not to deny the suicide's sin. It is to affirm the faith that was treasured by the suicide. What is more, you do not wish to deprive grieving families of the assurance that a Christian loved one is in heaven. Be that as it may, you wonder whether the concerns of the past ought not be today's concerns. Is it not fair to assert that by saying nothing about the sin of suicide during the service you may actually sanction suicide? I do not believe so. Speaking of the sin of the deceased does not deter people from committing suicide. It merely subjects the family to shame while it fuels the stigma of suicide.

Conclusion

Everyone in the church knows suicide is wrong. That is what makes the planning of a funeral service so difficult for pastors. You want to understand how something so devastating could take place under your watch. Please keep in mind that pastors are not immune to the ignorance that circulates following a suicide. Many fail to see the link between suicide and depression and for this reason continue to be influenced by the stigma that is associated with suicide. When a layperson expresses his ignorance, the stigma sounds something like this: "Others are able to snap out of their gloomy mood, why couldn't this person? Did he prefer being so sad? Was something wrong with him spiritually?" Pastors might be inclined to put a slightly different spin on it: "Why wasn't God's Word effective in this case? Did he fall away, having been driven to despair?" I understand such questions. It is not pleasant for pastors when we sense we are talking to a wall. We are in the business of saving souls, after all.

So how shall you respond one day when you are suddenly facing a funeral for a suicide? You were unable to make a given parishioner feel better, more appreciative of his Savior's forgiveness. What will you do now that he is dead? This question is long overdo, since Christians have never received a consistent response from the church on this issue. Suicide in the early church under the guise of martyrdom was followed by centuries of judgment and superstition. Today we are more knowledgeable concerning depression and mental illness. But the church has yet to put forward any practice that is unambiguous and biblical regarding the funeral of a suicide. Many pastors consequently have remained conspicuously silent at the time of the service, offering little or no encouragement to grieving believers. The reason for this is not difficult to understand. For centuries the church has spoken of Christian faith from a standpoint of human thinking and emotions rather than from a scriptural context. Today too faith is often seen from a rational perspective—what humans control—instead of as that which is from God. The result is that when a suicide takes place in the parish, the pastor is expected to make a judgment that he is not qualified to make. He must decide whether he will offer a Christian funeral based on what was this individual's motive for ending his life. What was going through this person's head?

You can be thankful that psychoanalyzing is not part of your job description. You are not called to cure the physically and emotionally ill. You are called to preach God's Word and administer the sacraments. And when parishioners are grieving because a fellow believer has taken his life, you are privileged to comfort those in trouble with the comfort you yourself have received from God (2 Corinthians 1:4).

Notes

[1]Edward Ellis and George Allen, *Traitor Within: Our Suicide Problem* (Garden City, NY: Doubleday and Company, Inc., 1961), p. 110.

[2]Augustine, *City of God,* edited by Philip Schaff, Vol. 2, *Nicene and Post-Nicene Fathers,* series 1 (Peabody, MA: Hendrickson Publishers, 1994), pp. 17,18. (Emphasis added by author.)

[3]Georges Minois, *History of Suicide: Voluntary Death in the Western World,* translated by Lydia G. Cochrane (Baltimore: Johns Hopkins University Press, 1995), p. 85.

[4]Ibid., pp. 31,32.

[5]Jeffrey R. Watt, *Choosing Death: Suicide and Calvinism in Modern Geneva* (Kirksville, MO: Truman State University Press, 2001), pp. 86,87.

[6]Minois, *History of Suicide*, p. 35.

[7]John H. C. Fritz, *Pastoral Theology* (St. Louis: Concordia Publishing House, 1945), p. 305.

[8]St. Nicholas Greek Orthodox Church of San Jose, CA, 1999–2006, http://www.saintni cholas.org/funerals.htm (accessed June 10, 2008).

Chapter 2

MODERN THEOLOGY AND A THRIVING STIGMA

Why Do the Paradoxes Concerning a Christian's Suicide Persist in the Church Today?

The doctrine during the Middle Ages that declared suicide an unforgivable sin had a discernible effect on the number of suicides among Christians. Suicides decreased considerably from the fourth to the seventh century. But there was a most regrettable cost, which the church has not overcome to this very day. It is known as suicide's stigma. In a matter of just a few centuries, suicide was no longer considered a convenient escape to heaven. It was the shortest highway to hell. Suicides were no longer designated martyrs for God but "martyrs for Satan." No longer was suicide the utmost proof of faith. It was proof that one had *given up* the faith. The number of suicides diminished, but the church had traded one dangerous doctrine for another. Instead of asserting that suicide was a means of grace, clergymen maintained it was the surest means of meeting God's judgment.

The study of psychology in recent decades has aided the church with respect to suicide's stigma. We understand that there is a correlation between suicide and mental illness, especially depression. This has resulted in the church changing its practices to some extent regarding the suicide of a Christian. The suicide may receive a Christian burial. Typically, the service can be held in the church. Nevertheless, the same fear persists among the clergy. If we state that the suicide was a Christian, we will make it easier for the next person who is troubled to follow suit. Presumably, if we come to understand what makes a suicide tick, we will condone the sin of suicide. Thus the church has not helped resolve the various paradoxes associated with suicide. Pastors have not helped remove from society the stigma associated with suicide. It may be noted, in fact, that the stigma is stronger in the church than anywhere else in our culture.

Much of the misinformation regarding Christians who commit suicide relates to a misconception of what it means to be a Christian. The misconception is supported by modern theology. In the chapters that follow, we will determine that we cannot resolve suicide's paradox without a proper understanding of faith. If the only question were, Is there forgiveness for the sin of suicide? one might deduce that all suicides go to heaven—a rather foolish conclusion. On the other hand, if the only question is, Was the person insane? that would compose another silly notion. Assuming that the majority of those who kill themselves are not insane, we might conclude that most people who commit suicide are lost.

The case against the believer who commits suicide will continue until the church as a whole adopts a more adequate understanding of Christian faith. What is the nature of faith? How does faith save? What is faith's source? When people lack an adequate understanding of faith, additional aspects of suicide's paradox are perceived, further inappropriate attempts are made at resolving the paradox, and the stigma surrounding a Christian's suicide remains in place.

The Nature of Faith

Christian faith is nothing more and nothing less than trust—trust in Christ as our Savior, trust in the forgiveness he earned for every sinner. Such faith may not be equated with positive feelings, cognitive thinking, reasonable opinions, or an understanding of truth. Such faith consists neither purely nor partially of human emotions or intellect. The nature of faith is that it receives. It receives the benefits of Christ's redemptive work on the cross. Faith does not look to itself or have faith as its object. Faith looks only to Christ, having Christ alone as its object. "Believe in the Lord Jesus, and you will be saved" (Acts 16:31).

How Faith Saves

Once we understand faith properly, it is important that we not attribute to faith what Scripture never attributes to it. Faith does not save on account of its nature, its attributes, or its strength. Neither does faith save because it is particularly trusting, exceptionally uncompromising, or especially strong or secure. Faith saves solely because of what it possesses, Christ and his forgiveness. "For we maintain that a man is justified by faith apart from observing the law" (Romans 3:28). By faith in Christ and his work of securing our forgiveness, we are declared righteous before God. This means that God, when looking at us, no longer sees the sinner. Instead, he sees his Son and Christ's righteousness. This is true despite the limitations of our faith. By faith in Christ we *have* Christ and therefore have his forgiveness.

The Source of Faith

Scripture is clear in its teaching that faith is a gift from God from start to finish. Faith is not generated by an exercise of the will. It is not initiated by some human activity. It is the Holy Spirit who enables us to trust in Christ and his work of redeeming sinners. Both the coming to such faith and the preservation of this faith is brought about not by individual ability or strength but entirely by the working of the Holy Spirit.[1] "No one can say, 'Jesus is Lord,' except by the Holy Spirit" (1 Corinthians 12:3).

If we have an accurate understanding of faith, we are less likely to be affected by suicide's stigma as it relates to believers who take their own lives. If we lack a right knowledge of faith, we are almost certain to be affected by suicide's stigma. What we may find most upsetting about the stigma relating to suicide is the presupposition that you cannot know for sure whether someone you have known your whole life to be a Christian died a Christian. This voiced ignorance, I believe, may be traced back to a presumption within the church that true Christian faith has a psychological basis. Knowingly, or unknowingly, people imply that Christian faith is dependent somehow on adequate mental health, rather than God's Word. If faith, however, is 100 percent from God the Holy Spirit and if we have confidence in his method of creating faith, we do not have to tiptoe around the subject of whether this person died a believer. Was he a believer *before* he developed clinical depression, before the delusional thinking set in, before he lost hope that he could change things and decided he was not worthy of life? Yes? Then we know the answer to whether he *died* a believer.

Natural Theology and Faith's "Add-Ons"

Whether you are a pastor or a Christian psychologist, you may be of the same opinion. Even the most acute case of depression does not pose some unavoidable threat upon one's faith in Christ. Depression does not have that kind of power. It may attack one's take on life or one's assessment of self-worth. However, it does not attack one's faith. But what if depression or the loss of hope is followed by suicide? What if we can see a correlation between that illness, that sense of desperation, and that decision to end one's life? The paradox to which we turn in the following chapters is the more general question of whether faith and suicide can appear in the same sentence.

In former days, suicide's stigma was fed by various radical doctrines within the church. In recent years, it is the church at large that has sustained the stigma. I believe it is the result of pastors buying in to a noteworthy breed of *natural theology*. Natural theology is what you end up with when you rely on reason rather than Scripture for an understanding of God and God's relationship with a fallen human race. The theology presupposes that there is a God, but it does not presuppose that man is a sinner and therefore cannot sustain a relationship with God without God's intervention. Obviously all theology, whether supported by Scripture or not, is premised by a natural knowledge of God. You do not have to be a Christian to believe that there is a god. Everyone is born with a conscience, which informs us inasmuch as there is a difference between right and wrong that there is someone over us and to whom we are accountable. That someone is God. Everyone can also observe the wonders of creation and be convinced that there is a Creator. What is different about natural theology is that it assumes we may obtain the truth about how we are deemed acceptable to God without receiving any communication from God.

Churches that are traditionally conservative in their teachings will ordinarily steer clear of such theology. However, when forced to respond to something as dreadful and scandalous as suicide, many pastors, I am afraid, become vulnerable to some aspects of it. This is *very* unfortunate, for anytime you mix natural theology with Christianity, it will have an unfavorable effect on how the church understands faith and Christians who struggle with mental illness.

To be a bit more specific, much of today's stigma associated with suicide corresponds to several false teachings regarding Christian faith. In each case we may refer to them as faith's "add-ons."[2] It is not that we can observe them as official doctrines of any particular denomination. The clergy, for the most part, I'm sure do not even verbalize such teachings. I believe the thinking is fostered more generally in various and subtle ways among the laity, who may lack a clear understanding of the nature of faith and how it saves. However, the clergy are quick to promote the beliefs when faced with a paradox they haven't the theological skill to resolve. In this way, the thinking of countless Christians has been conditioned by what reason or a natural knowledge of God deduces in the wake of a suicide. People have preconceived ideas about how true faith will perform in a given case. Popular opinion is that we can feel good about our faith or perhaps someone else's faith as long as certain standards are maintained and the Christian community is able to pick up on them. We choose good over evil. We understand and are able to articulate our appreciation for God's grace. We demonstrate an enthusiasm for serving in our various vocations. We are always optimistic concerning the future. And what if we do not maintain these standards? The church today will do well to be informed. If true Christian faith is something more than trusting in our only Savior's forgiveness, if it is generated and sustained by something in the individual rather than by the gospel, if it saves because of what we are able to do with it instead of what it possesses, it will be much easier to judge the suicide as a person who gave up the faith.

Notes

[1]Formula of Concord, Solid Declaration, II:25-27, *The Book of Concord: The Confessions of the Evangelical Lutheran Church,* translated and edited by Theodore G. Tappert (Philadelphia: Fortress Press, 1959), p. 526.

[2]My first comments on faith and its faulty definitions is referenced in an article I wrote for *Family Talk,* Vol. 8, No. 2 (Winter 2006).

Chapter 3

FAITH PLUS OBEDIENCE

 Christians "turn from evil and do good" (Psalm 34:14). Yet this Christian chose suicide!

Shawn is a bachelor and has never expressed any regrets about it. Over the years it has permitted him to be extremely active in the congregation, volunteering to help at every possible opportunity. However, it has been some time since you last saw him at a service and even longer since he has attended the monthly meeting of the trustees. A friend of his, and fellow parishioner, has recently informed you that he was fired this past week, after serving the company faithfully for 25 years. You decide to phone him for some answers and to hopefully offer him some encouragement. Your call wakens Shawn from an afternoon nap. You don't get him to say much, and it's evident he's not taking your call very seriously. Yes, he lost his job, but everything is fine. He'll see you next Sunday.

A couple weeks go by, and you receive some more reports from his friend. Shawn has become increasingly withdrawn. He has no time for social events and hasn't been returning anyone's calls. Furthermore, he refuses to leave his apartment, sleeping half the day away. In general, he lacks initiative, will not follow through with any commitments, and appears apathetic about everything.

That was yesterday. Today Shawn's friend has phoned you from the hospital with news of Shawn's suicide. How do you respond?

We may regard it as a most troubling custom within the church: in order to resolve suicide's paradox, we redefine faith. We formulate our doctrine not on the basis of Scripture but on natural theology. Faith's first add-on has to do with obedience and choices that are made from an obedient heart. It is believed that Christians will not do certain things. Christians will never murder, commit adultery, steal, or be seduced into idolatrous practices. Genuine Christians, moreover, do not commit suicide. A true believer loves God's commandments and makes choices in life in conformity to his commandments. It provides an easy resolution to the paradox. Apparently this person therefore who *did* take his life was not a Christian. He must not have had a genuine faith.

Can a Christian Choose What He Knows to Be Wicked?

Shawn was very deliberate with regard to life's decisions. Some would call him precise. This was especially true when he knew a given choice of his would affect those he served. Sometimes he would spend hours plotting out a given assignment before following through. This had earned for him a reputation both in the parish and at work for being a very selfless individual. Today, on the other hand, his behavior appeared extremely selfish. Some would say he was thinking only of himself.

If you have been in the ministry for some time, you are sure to have preached on the point. Christians choose to do things they know they should not and which prove unfortunate and disastrous. Having faith in Christ does not provide a remedy for the sinful nature. As a preacher, your words leave no room for misunderstanding. Every believer is a sinner. Apart from faith, one is predisposed to choose what is wrong and consequently evil in God's eyes. The Lord has told us this in no uncertain terms; every inclination of man's heart is evil from childhood (Genesis 8:21). Every believer likewise will *remain* a sinner throughout his pilgrimage here on earth.

If people miss the mark on what it means to be a sinner, they run the risk of misinterpreting what constitutes true faith. For many professing to be Christian, faith approaches the idea of obedience. Faith is seen as a person's response to the gospel, which is trust in God's mercy, but at the same time also as a response to the commandments.[1] Faith is seen as the equivalent of having made a moral choice. In fact, choice by some is regarded as that which gives birth to faith. The implications of this assertion, however, are quite troubling. If making the right choice, a *good* choice, is how you become a *believer,* then making the wrong choice, a *bad* choice, is how you become an *unbeliever.* But which wrong choice? Who's to say? To play it safe, perhaps for every wrong choice a person makes there should be a remedying right choice in order to remain in the faith. This is absurd, of course, and is not possible for *any* believer. As human beings who are constantly sinning, we are thus constantly making wrong choices.

It goes with being a sinner. You are faced very suddenly with a difficult choice, and you are not sure which way to go. Proving especially regrettable or tragic is when you change your entire life with one poor choice. As a young employee, you tell your boss where he can go, and you are immediately fired, ruining any chance of moving up in the company. As a brand-new father, you spend a night drinking, get into an accident on your way home, and in a single moment alter the lives of your entire family. As a straight-A student in high school, you spend one evening with the wrong date. You conceive a beautiful child, but also lose an opportunity to take advantage of a several thousand-dollar scholarship. Shawn's single but costly choice was to put an end to his difficulties. The price was his life.

Believers and nonbelievers alike are capable of making disastrous choices. Like the nonbeliever you may also pay the price. This does not mean, however, that you will also perish like the nonbeliever. Coming to mind is Lot's wife, whose sinful choice resulted in her death. Lot and his family were warned by two angels to flee from the wicked city of Sodom and not to look back (Genesis 19:17). In the last moments, however, Lot's wife *did* look back, and she became a pillar of salt (Genesis 19:26). Did she go to hell? Scripture does not indicate that she did. We are simply informed that she lost her life. Luther proposes she may have believed the danger had elapsed once she came from the city into the open country.[2] Perhaps she was like the curious child on Christmas morning who convinces himself that one little peek under the wrapping paper won't harm anyone. Perhaps she coveted her former life and in a moment of weakness chose to test her Lord. Lot's wife was a believer. There are, however, temporal consequences to losing sight of God's commands. And so she was changed into a pillar of salt.[3] Like Shawn, who committed suicide, Lot's wife was disobedient. And it cost her her life.

Some people pay a higher price for their devastating choices in life than do others. Fortunately, faith is not about making one choice or many choices. Faith is about trusting in *God's* choice to send his only begotten Son to die for us sinners. It is imperative that every Christian pastor make this teaching of faith a priority, for this reason. As one choice does not create faith, neither does one choice destroy faith. What destroys faith is being cut off from that which creates faith. Faith cannot stand up to the deliberate welcoming of a sin, which leads one away from the Word of God. Jesus informed the disciples: "You are already clean because of the word I have spoken to you" (John 15:3). Then, referring to his same Word he says, "Remain in me, and I will remain in you" (John 15:4). This Christ promises to every believer. Through his message of salvation, you will remain in

41

faith. The flip side of this is obvious: "If anyone does not remain in me [in my Word], he is like a branch that is thrown away and withers" (John 15:6). Apart from the gospel, faith cannot survive. So what about the faith of the person who chooses suicide? Concerning Shawn, who remained faithful both in his service to the church and in attendance at weekly services, we may assume the following: while taking his life was an unfortunate choice—a fatal choice, in fact—it was not a choice with eternal consequences.

There is another risk in defining true faith in connection with right choices. You undermine the function of faith. Scriptures teach that the sinner is justified by faith alone. It is imperative that those called to teach how sinners are saved understand this. If one is not saved by faith alone, it will be that which is added to faith that does the saving. It will be one's love, one's observance of God laws, or one's pious choices that save. But that is not what Christians believe. The church believes that salvation is by grace through faith and nothing above and beyond faith. Indeed, this faith never exists by itself because good works are sure to follow.

Unfortunately, there are many in the church today who are uncomfortable when good works are made to take a backseat. The preferred opinion in some circles is that faith is not enough to save or justify, *not* unless it is reinforced by the right behavior. The belief is that faith justifies not because it possesses Christ's forgiveness but because by faith the believer is enabled to live a new life of obedience.[4] This teaching, however, forces *faith* to take a backseat concerning our salvation. And this is an impossible thing for faith. The reformer Martin Luther once had this to say about faith: "Faith in its proper function has no other object than Jesus Christ, the Son of God, who was put to death for the sins of the world. It does not look at its love and say: 'What have I done? Where have I sinned? What have I deserved?' But it says: 'What has Christ done? What has He deserved?'"[5] It is because Christ is the *object* of your faith that you can be sure you have *true* faith.

Faith is not a work that a believer performs. Faith simply lets God be God. It does not *give* to God. It *receives* from God. Understanding faith this way is what allows you as a believer to be sure you are going to heaven. If faith consisted in part of Christian obedience or making proper choices, you could have no such confidence. Your choices, which are polluted every day by sin, would only cause you to question whether your faith was lacking in some way. Similarly, when we tack something on to faith and how faith saves, we are not permitted to know whether a suicide went to heaven. We may only speculate as to whether or not his faith faltered in the end. When faith, however, stands alone as trust in Christ and his gift for forgiveness, we may offer comfort to the survivors of a suicide who was a Christian.

So is the case with Shawn's family. How you respond to his suicide will be determined by the faith he confessed and demonstrated throughout his baptized life.

Notes

[1]Hermann Sasse, *Here We Stand: Nature and Character of the Lutheran Faith* (St. Louis: Concordia Publishing House, 1938), p. 122.

[2]Martin Luther, *Luther's Works,* edited by Jaroslav Pelikan and Helmut T. Lehmann, American Edition, Vol. 3, Lectures on Genesis Chapters 15-20 (St. Louis: Concordia Publishing House; Philadelphia: Fortress Press, 1955–1986), p. 298.

[3]Ibid.

[4]Martin Chemnitz, *Justification,* translated by J. A. O. Preus (St. Louis: Concordia Publishing House, 1946) p. 84.

[5]*Luther's Works,* Vol. 26, p. 88.

Chapter 4

FAITH PLUS REASON

Christians know that God cares for every one of his creatures (Psalm 145:16). Yet this Christian concluded that suicide was the answer!

You have known Mary since she attended Sunday school nearly 30 years ago. Since then, she has confided in you on various occasions with regard to her family as well as the parish. She knows she can visit with you about sensitive issues. Additionally, up until now, what she has related to you has not seemed particularly unusual. That is, until you visit her in the hospital one day. Entering her room, it is immediately evident that she is confused and afraid. She doesn't know why her husband has brought her to this place. She belongs at home where she can take care of her baby. "Bruce says I've been scaring little Kelly. I should let him take care of her for a while."

When Mary's husband phoned you from the hospital earlier, he expressed a concern that his wife might hurt their child. Mary had been irritable and mean around him for a number of weeks. What if she took it out on their daughter?

Bruce's fears are soon reinforced from your perspective. Mary's analysis of things clearly is not normal. "I know my husband has been talking to the staff here. They want to take my baby away from me. But you have to understand. I'm just trying to protect her!" At this point, Mary shares some very disturbing thoughts with you. She asserts that the Lord has sent a demon to torment her. Moreover, if she's not extremely careful, the demon may possess her girl.

That was three weeks ago. Today you receive word that it perhaps wasn't the baby who was in the greatest danger, but the baby's mother. Back at home Mary has taken her own life. How will you help the survivors make sense out of their loss?

It is something you may not begin to comprehend: how a fellow believer would deem suicide the logical answer to his difficulties. You may find even more troubling, however, another false doctrine regarding the nature of Christian faith. Once again I bring to your attention a teaching that is based not on Scripture but natural theology. As the church strives to resolve suicide's paradox, we observe a second add-on to Christian faith. The paradox is resolved, apparently, if you observe a given relationship between faith and reason. It is asserted that Christians will not draw certain conclusions. A true believer, for example, will not determine "My life is hopeless. Even God is against me. I'd be better off dead." To assume that true believers cannot deduce certain things, however, is to assume that the mentally ill may have an ill faith or even no faith at all.

Can a Christian *believe* as he should if he cannot *reason* as he should?

At Mary's funeral when people ask how she died and you explain that she took her life, they don't have to say out loud what they are thinking. You can see the look of horror and shock on their faces, and you know what is going through their minds. Why? Of all people, how could Mary even think of doing such a thing? If they knew Mary, what they were really asking is, How can any believer conclude that suicide is the answer?

A Place for Reason

People often imagine that when wrong deductions lead to wrong and tragic choices, there is only one explanation. The heart is wrong. It simply is not possible for a Christian to reason that suicide under given circumstances may be a viable option! If shameful thoughts assumed command of their *actions,* surely the same thoughts assumed command of their *faith.*

We need to distinguish, however, between what faith *is* and what someone with faith *determines* in a given situation. Christian faith is trust. You trust in Christ your Savior for the forgiveness of sins. You trust that his punishment on the cross was sufficient in securing eternal life for sinners. Faith is not the same thing as one's ability to engage in flawless reasoning: if God promises to care for his *entire creation,* he will certainly take care of *me.* True faith, rather, clings to Christ despite how futile this clinging may seem under the circumstances. In this sense, faith defies logic. Faith trusts in Christ, even when, according to the faulty thinking of the believer, such trusting makes no sense.

Reason, nevertheless, has a definite role in the life of a believer. When you preach or confess the Christian faith, reason serves the hearer by means of God's Word. Through the process of reason, God's Word guides the believer, so that he might live in accordance with his faith. *And* when he fails in this regard, his reason convicts him, communicating the truth about his sin. Moreover, when the same Scriptures communicate that Christ's blood has atoned for the world's sin, the hearer's reason communicates that the Lamb of God has covered his sin. He may believe he is redeemed and stands without fault in God's sight.

God has designed reason so that it may serve the believer. Reason, however, cannot prove beneficial to your faith apart from the Holy Spirit and God's Word. When operating independently, reason merely concludes: "Sin is good, and I don't need God" and persuades you to do what will serve your own selfish interests. Apart from God's Word, reason may furthermore presume: "I must fix what is wrong in this world of mine. And if I cannot, nor can those around me, then this world is not worth my time and trouble."

When operating under the supervision of the Word, however, your reason will serve your Christian faith by making your faith capable of observing God's gifts in this life. You might say that reason is like a mirror. Reason offers an image of God's blessings. It permits you to reflect on everything Christ has gained for sinners and how you as a believer obtain God's gifts. You reflect on the truth that our gracious God and Savior is slow to anger and abounding in love and faithfulness (Psalm 86:15). You reflect on the fact that you have faith and that through faith you have the forgiveness of sins that Christ earned for you on the cross.

Under normal circumstances, reason is a valuable servant to faith. Your reason tells you, "Go to the Word. That is where God will deliver you!" But what if your reason is not telling you what it should? To be sure, reason will serve faith so long as the believer hears God's Word and is capable of reflecting on the blessings God reserves for believers. However, what about those who are not capable of reflecting on the blessings of God? Because of an illness of some kind, their reason has been impaired, depriving them of the ability to think rationally. Perhaps they have even lost contact with reality. You may think of that antique mirror you have stored away in your home somewhere. It once offered a perfect reflection to the individual who stood before it, looking at his image. Today the image is cloudy and warped from being exposed to extreme heat and temperature changes over the years. Sadly, the mirror is no longer able to offer an accurate picture of the viewer. So it is for the Christian whose thoughts are distorted on account of an ailing mind. His reason is no longer capable of communicating a true image of God's gifts in his life. What shall we make of him who is no longer able to reflect properly on God's blessings? Yes, he has lost a servant. But has he lost his faith? By no means!

Delusional Thinking

Prior to her suicide, there were times when Mary had a complete break with reality. Normal thinking was replaced with an assortment of fantasies. The demon she had concocted was informing her of an increasing number of acquaintances who were out to get her, destroy her reputation, hence her life. How might she have reacted if you had asked her what God thought of this horrific situation? Would he "who did not spare his own Son, but gave him up for us all— . . . not also, along with him, graciously give us all things?" (Romans 8:32). Mary might not have reflected a whole lot on the implications of Christ's death for her present situation. All she could think about was the growing number of enemies she had made who would surely get their way. She felt as though God had given up jurisdiction over her life.

The delusions of some, to be sure, will prove more bizarre and creative than those of others. However, it is a common dilemma, a perception that is familiar in far too many cases. The troubled Christian is convinced his life and many blessings have been ripped from God's gracious care. To say nothing about God's purposes, the Lord simply is not going to help in this instance. The believer may not be rational, but this is what he knows. It is not that he is no longer willing to reflect on God's goodness and grace. He simply is unable to. All evidence of God's blessings has been removed from his life.

For some it will seem like an obvious question: Have those who have lost the ability to reason properly lost something elemental to faith? We answer with a simple truth: reason may *serve* faith, but it does not *create* faith. Reason is not to be *equated* with faith. Reason may enable a believer to *appreciate* what it means to be a believer, but reason is not what *makes* a believer a believer. Faith is neither obtained nor sustained by human reason. The ability to reason is not what causes a person to have faith in his Savior. Perhaps no one has articulated it better than Martin Luther. He writes: "I believe that I cannot by my own reason or strength believe in Jesus Christ, my Lord, or come to him; but the Holy Spirit has called me by the Gospel."[1] Faith is not a result of *any* human effort or activity. Faith is God's doing and his alone.

This is the issue following the suicide of a Christian. Of greatest importance is not what this person *understood* about true faith. What is important in every case is what a person *has* by faith, namely, forgiveness and eternal life. You may think about an infant who is given a rattle. With every finger on his hand, he latches on to the little toy. His grip leaves no question as to whether the little plaything is in his possession. The baby has his rattle without being cognizant of the fact. The little one's grip illustrates an important truth about faith. If a child can have all the benefits of faith without understanding the facts of faith, an adult can too. There is great comfort in this truth. It matters very little whether you are a baptized infant, an Alzheimer's patient, or someone who is suffering from delusional thinking. Your faith may lack awareness or understanding. But it does not lack forgiveness or salvation.

Sound reason is neither a prerequisite to Christian faith nor does it in some manner complete faith. Sometimes listening to human reason, in fact, *cannot* serve us. Although guided by Scripture, reason on occasion has its limits. Your reason may function in a perfectly healthy manner but stand in complete opposition to God's Word. That is what Abraham came to understand one day when tested by God. Although he was perfectly sane, his reason would absolutely betray him. God promised Abraham that the Messiah would come from his seed. In time God gave Abraham his firstborn, Isaac. Isaac was also Abraham's only child. But then God commanded Abraham to sacrifice his only son, Isaac. And Abraham was faced with a horrible paradox. Could God really demand such a thing? Apart from Isaac, there was no seed, no future Messiah, no Savior, nor would there ever be. So what was Abraham to deduce? Was God lying when he promised to bless him through Isaac? Was the command to sacrifice Isaac not from God but rather from the devil?[2]

Abraham may be likened to an individual who is mentally ill. There was a time in the patriarch's life when human reason could not serve him as he sought to trust in God. However, he never faltered in his faith. Despite what his reason was telling him, Abraham trusted in God's promise and would let God's promise stand. Even in the midst of what appeared to be a horrible contradiction, he believed in God's compassion—that the Lord would never go back on his Word. Abraham also believed there was a reason for this test and in time everything would become clear to him. Perhaps he would sacrifice the traditional offering in place of his son, a lamb for the

49

burnt offering (Genesis 22:7). For a time, of course, it was a mystery as to where Abraham might find such a lamb.

Sometimes faith must live with a paradox. Faith must believe in God's compassionate care even when one's life seems to be going down the drain and the Lamb is apparently nowhere in sight. The thing is, faith may have no choice in the matter. Faith does not believe *so long* as it sees the Lamb and God's diagram for the future. Rather, faith believes *despite* what it sees because it clings to God's Word, whose promises never change.

This is true regardless of the extent to which reason is serving the troubled believer. If you are mentally healthy and yet are confronted with a crisis, it may be just a moment's time and you see the Lamb. Life's paradox is resolved when you hear the gospel preached to you on Sunday morning. You remember your baptism, which washes away life's many offenses. You see Christ's body and blood in the sacrament, which atoned for the sins of the world. The mentally troubled may sometimes spend days, weeks, or even months, waiting for a clear picture of the Lamb. To a certain extent that is what contributed to Mary's sense of desperation. Where was Jesus when she needed him the most? How she longed for some reassuring message from his Word! But all she could hear were these voices from hell. In some cases, life's paradox is never resolved in the minds of those who are disturbed. However, it is not the *length* one waits that is relevant. What is relevant is *that* one waits. And thankfully, it is not reason that enables one to wait. It is faith, God's perfect gift.

It becomes a dangerous business when we regard reason as a requirement for faith. We make faith dependent not on God's gift but on that which has been contaminated by sin. Such faith is doomed from the start. There is no exception. Faith that relies on reason will be corrupted by reason. This is why, in the words of Luther, "you must let reason go. It must be killed and buried in believers."[3] In doing so, you will, in fact, "kill a beast that is greater than the world."[4] No wonder when Solomon instructs you to trust in the Lord with all your heart, that he warns you to lean *not* on your own understanding (Proverbs 3:5). If you rely on your own understanding, you are relying on that which is bound to drive you away from the Word so that you lose our faith.

This is not to say, however, that reason, which "takes a leave of absence," has abandoned God's Word. It has abandoned the believer. The disturbed Christian has not forsaken Scripture. He has been forsaken by an illness. This you must know about the believer: an illness can impair reason, but impaired reason does not prevent God from giving and sustaining faith. God's Word is more powerful than your reason, and God can give faith through his Word without the help of your reason.

A sick mind does not represent a sick faith. The mind that is ill has merely been altered. Its perception of God's earthly blessings has changed. In a dream you might envision that your house has been vandalized and that all of your most precious belongings have been destroyed. For the severely depressed, this in fact is what has happened to his life. The average onlooker may see that everything in this person's life is still in place, but in the mind of the sick individual, it has all been ravaged and ruined beyond repair. Can a person still have faith when every indication is that the daily blessings of his Lord have fled from his life? Yes, he can, because Christian faith is not the ability to understand or rationalize. Faith is neither seeing nor perceiving. It is trust.

When we add on to faith, we may not know whether the Christian who dies by his own hand was saved. However, the decision to kill oneself is not a decision based on a malfunctioning faith. It is based to a large degree on faulty information. Unyielding depression has advised the ailing Christian that he is worthless and unserviceable. Moreover, he assumes that God feels the same way about him. God's Word, however, has a greater say than the inner accusations spawned by a sinner's illness. And the verdict is in. "Who will bring any charge against those whom God has chosen? It is God who justifies" (Romans 8:33). The final word concerning faith remains unchanged for the irrational and mentally ill. Faith does not reason why. It trusts. The believer is saved by faith, but not because this faith is still capable of reasonable thought. We are saved because of what we *possess* by faith—the forgiveness our Savior secured for us on the cross.

In the end, that is how you help the survivors make sense out of Mary's suicide. Although they may never comprehend how Mary could conceive the need for taking such measures, they can be sure she was a Christian. She never let go of the eternal treasures she held by faith in Christ.

Notes

[1]*Luther's Small Catechism With Explanation* (St. Louis: Concordia Publishing House, 1986), p. 15.

[2]*Luther's Works,* Vol. 4, p. 95.

[3]*What Luther Says: An Anthology,* compiled by Ewald M. Plass, 3 vols. (St. Louis: Concordia Publishing House, 1959), no. 1440, p. 485.

[4]*Luther's Works,* Vol. 26, p. 228.

Chapter 5

FAITH PLUS SELF-ESTEEM

Depressive illnesses often affect not simply the ability to reason, what one perceives about the world, but also what is perceived about oneself. Placed in jeopardy is one's *self-esteem*, to use a popular term of the day.[1] Self-esteem consists of a personal evaluation of whether others *accept* you and whether you are *worthy* to be loved. It is strongly related to how you believe you are viewed by important others in your life.[2] Suicide often occurs when the depressed individual is robbed of a sense of identity and value to others. He simply will not be persuaded that he can or ever will contribute anything to the lives of others. It often comes down to whether he is able to believe in himself.

 Scripture promises that everyone who believes in Christ "will never be put to shame" (Romans 9:33). Yet this Christian could not even believe in himself.

Dennis' wife moved in with her mother, telling him before she left that she was unable to deal any longer with his bouts of silence. For days at a time he would become disengaged and impossible to talk to. "Things will never get better if you don't tell me what's bothering you," she told him. Finally, she phones you to fill you in on matters and later stops by your office. "He's down on everything, making me unhappy just being in the same room with him!" she complains. "I think he's suffering from depression and needs help. But he won't hear of it!" At first she thought he was simply having some bad days at work. "One day he would suddenly seem very sad. A few days later he would be better. More recently, however, he has become very despondent. It is also apparent that he feels ashamed about something."

This does not surprise you. In a conversation with Dennis the previous day, he had tossed out this question: "Why would she even want to give me a second chance? I certainly don't deserve it. I hope she leaves me. Heaven knows even I don't want to be around myself."

You never were able to pry out of Dennis what seemed to be weighing on him so heavily. One thing was clear. He hated who he was and who he would remain. It was, in fact, more than he could cope with. This led to regular drinking binges, a couple of which landed him in the county jail, and the inability to function adequately either at work or at home.

That was last month. Today you hear that Dennis has ended his misery by way of suicide. What shall you say to his family?

Another add-on to Christian faith surfaces among those who try to resolve suicide's great paradox. It is advanced by a third false teaching about faith that finds its starting point in natural theology. It is presumed that believing in *oneself* is a prerequisite to believing in *Christ*—that in order to possess the *Holy* Spirit, you must have a healthy *human* spirit. This ridiculous belief, I believe, is fueled by the great emphasis these days placed on self-esteem. People recall that this believer—before he took his life—lacked a motivation to take on life's tasks. He kept skipping work, calling in sick. He wasn't around when family or close acquaintances wanted to reach him. He complained that people deserved better than the likes of him. They were better off going somewhere else for help. "Just leave me alone!" was his answer when people showed some concern. And because you cannot force someone to accept your help, he eventually *was* for the most part left alone to work out his troubles. Unfortunately, that is when he took his life.

How could this fellow Christian do such a thing? The paradox is resolved when you are allowed to presume something. An unhealthy self-esteem is indicative of an unhealthy faith. In other words, unless this person has the same opinion of himself as God has, his faith cannot be what it should be. Therefore, the only explanation for his suicide is that he lost his faith. This argument, however, fails to distinguish between faith and self-esteem, that is, between faith in Christ and self-faith. True faith is trust. It takes aim not at oneself but directly at Christ and his work of redeeming sinners. It trusts in Christ even though in so doing the believer must trust in Christ over and against himself. Whether you have faith, therefore, is not determined by your current level of self-esteem but by whether you have confidence in Christ's forgiveness for the world. Faith is not confidence in oneself but is confidence in the gospel, how God saves sinners.

Self-Esteem and Believing in Oneself

Can a Christian believe in *Christ* if he cannot believe in *himself?*

It was a process Dennis' wife did not pick up on for some time: his loss of self-esteem and his inability to believe in himself. In time he was utterly convinced that he was a failure, both as a husband and as a father. During the little time you were permitted to visit with Dennis, you argued that nothing major has changed since his depression first waged its assault. He is still the loving and gifted individual he has always been. But he doesn't buy it. He is feeling revulsion toward himself. And he is convinced others will find a basis for it. He's thinking: "Nothing I do will benefit my family and friends and others whom I love and respect! God cannot possibly use me to benefit those who make up my life!"

How do you console the family whose loved one opts to die because he apparently felt he lacked importance? It may help to compare depression, which often proves incurable and precedes suicide, to a slow progressive cancer. Like a growing malignant tumor attacks a given organ of the body, depression eats away at one's sense of worth as an individual. You may comfort Dennis' wife by helping her recognize something very basic concerning Christian faith. A Christian absolutely may believe in Christ while having a complete lack of self-faith. True faith concerns one's Savior and what *he* has done for the world, not what the Christian perceives *he* is able to do. The effect of severe depression, for that reason, is not necessarily of concern to the Christian, not with respect to his faith anyway.

Having said that, how important is it to believe in oneself? Self-faith, to be sure, has great value in one's life. For one thing, it gives you a reason for fulfilling your different vocations and to do so on a daily basis. You expect to experience a given amount of joy and satisfaction in serving those whom God has assigned to you as your particular responsibility. Additionally, and more to the point, is the fact that the loss of self-esteem may prove a serious threat to your physical well-being. I am referring to the obvious link that depressive illnesses and the loss of self-esteem have with suicide.

Severe clinical depression may in some instances be termed a *terminal* illness, but not because a medical diagnosis of the person's state would ever assert this. It is not that the depressed individual can offer any evidence that he is going to die. Looking back *after* the fact, however, we are able to establish a relationship between depression, suicidal thinking, and finally the suicidal act. Much like a cancer patient who dies despite his treatments, so is the person suffering from major depression apt to die inasmuch as his depression is "untreatable." In time his illness eats away at his sense of worth; self-esteem is replaced with self-loathing; he deems he is nothing to the world; he is garbage, as far as God is concerned; and it is time to die. And, sadly, despite any relevant prognosis that says he is dying, he does die, be it by his own hand.

You would never propose, to be sure, that suicides be explained away as resulting from a disease and say nothing about sin. What you may assume is that Christians do not commit suicide because in some tragic way they lost their faith in Christ. They lost faith in themselves. There is no apparent relationship between suicide and the rejection of Christ. Where you observe a relationship is between one's self-esteem and one's will to live and between one's loss of self-esteem and one's will to die.

Self-Esteem and One's Identity as a Christian

Prior to Dennis' illness, he never lacked a sense of who he was as an individual. He served in various vocations but was first and foremost a Christian husband and father. After his depression robbed him of his identity (as he had perceived it), he obtained a boost in his self-esteem when for a short period his medication started working. He made the decision to return to college for one more semester to earn an elementary education degree. His intention was to serve as a parochial school teacher in the upper grades. After a few days, however, things took a regrettable turn. Dennis' depression returned, his self-esteem vanished, and he never recovered.

The benefits of self-esteem are limited. A healthy self-esteem may supply the desire to live out one's life, but it does not help one live a *Christian* life. It does not indicate whether somebody truly loves God and is interested in carrying out the vocations into which God has placed him. One person may have an extremely healthy self-esteem because of what he perceives others think of him and yet have no desire to live as a Christian. Another person, who is very sincere about his Christian life, may have very little self-esteem to speak of because of how he perceives others view him. Both should know what really matters is not whether one is able, with the help of others, to believe in oneself, but whether by the help of the Holy Spirit one is able to believe in Christ. Unfortunately, neither individual may take into account what God says about him.

At this point, you may ask whether *self-esteem* is the most appropriate term to use. What is more important, what your neighbor *believes* about you or what your God *says* about you? It is normal within any given culture to believe in yourself, having obtained some positive feedback from those around you. Your self-esteem teaches you to consult with those whom you are called to serve, in order to perform a kind of self-analysis. A couple terms I prefer over *self-esteem* are *self-regard* and *self-worth*. These terms help you base your identity less on how you *appear* and more on who you *are*. How you see yourself ought to have less to do with the perception of a select few and more to do with what God had in mind when he created you. Of course, there is a problem you incur with the use of these terms from the very start. If the *regard* or *worth* you have for yourself is based on who you really are, then you must establish who you are from God's standpoint. The problem with this is that God says you are a sinner. Who you are by nature is one who stands condemned before your Creator and divine judge.

This problem is resolved, however, when the Christian observes the blessings he has by faith in Christ and how they far exceed those that are obtained by faith in oneself. One author explains this at some length as he substitutes for the term *self-esteem* the term *Christ-esteem*. The former, which is based on humanistic psychology, would have you know yourself so that you might *feel good* about yourself. The latter, which is based on biblical Christianity, would have you know yourself so that you might *turn away from* yourself and discover your life and identify in Christ Jesus.[3] Since the sinner is the problem, developing self-esteem and focusing attention on yourself is not the solution to your human dilemma but merely compounds the problem.[4] Instead, you must deny yourself. When you look to yourself, you see your sin. When you look away from yourself and to the righteousness of Christ, which God imputes to you, you see your new identity.[5] In the words of the apostle, "Therefore, if anyone is in Christ, he is a new creation; the old has gone, the new has come!" (2 Corinthians 5:17).

Your new identity in Christ is what finally allows you to believe without any doubt that you have worth. More important than your ability for self-love or fastening some value on yourself is how you are loved and valued by God. Your Savior suffered death on a cross so that you may appear without blemish in the sight of God. What's more, despite how your life might change over time, nothing can change God's declaration! One moment, to be sure, could deprive you of your health. A physical disability could result in people placing less value on your services. A mental disability or a change in circumstances could deprive you of your desire to believe in yourself and retain an active role in other people's lives. However, even if, in your opinion, you become the most detestable creature on earth, nothing can deprive you of your identity in Christ. You and I are blameless children of God through the redeeming blood of our Savior.

When Self-Esteem Is Given Too Much Attention

Another problem occurs when people confuse self-faith with Christian faith. In addition to causing people to misjudge an individual, it may cause an individual to misjudge himself. And this can prove disastrous. Recall the disciple Peter and his great boast to stand by his Lord. Jesus had predicted that Peter would deny him three times. But Peter insisted: "Even if all fall away on account of you, I never will. . . . Even if I have to die with you, I will never disown you" (Matthew 26:33,35). Peter could just as well have said, "Bring it on! I'm ready for anything!" Unfortunately, his booming self-esteem did not prevent Jesus' words from proving true. Peter's confessed faith in himself did not help him in the final hour to confess his faith in Christ when the moment of truth arrived. Peter mistook his high opinion of himself for faith in his Savior.

The disciple Peter may serve as a valuable lesson for people today who confuse self-esteem with Christian faith. While there is some benefit in having faith in yourself, it is both dangerous and unwise to have faith in your faith, that is, faith in your own ability to believe in Christ and remain faithful to him. The proverb reads, "He who trusts in himself is a fool" (Proverbs 28:26). That was Peter's problem. He had *too much* faith in himself, so much that he relied on himself to stand by his confession rather than on Christ. And he set himself up for a humiliating fall.

Peter bet his entire future with Christ on self-faith, what you might also call courage. Unfortunately, when Peter found himself in over his head, there was nothing his courage could do to help him profess his Savior's name.

That is not to say that courage is undesirable. Certainly, every believer would rather show courage than cowardice. You no doubt will prefer confessing the faith, despite the offense you are sure to cause, to giving your Savior a bad name. And if it came to it, you would hope to defend Christ's truth no matter what it cost you, even if it meant dying for his truth. As for the extremely depressed believer, he would hope to do the same. He would hope to confess the faith and advance the same faith by his Christian life, even if it meant, in his case, living instead of dying. If you could choose the final outcome in a given instance, you would choose to be courageous every time.

But what does it mean to be strong as a Christian? Real faith has nothing to do with accessing your human strength. Christian faith has to do with accessing Christ. Martin Luther says about saving faith that it does not look at its works or at its own strength and worthiness, but goes outside of itself, clinging to Christ and embracing him as its own possession.

To summarize, confusing self-esteem or courage with faith can meet with grave disappointment when a person develops a cocky outlook on life and then falls flat on his face. An equally heartbreaking scenario exists for one who has no self-esteem to speak of and is of the misguided notion that he somehow has gone wrong spiritually.

Dennis, you had learned, was confusing the loss of self-worth with the loss of faith. When his depression reached perhaps its most intolerable level, he commented to his sister that he was afraid he was losing his faith. "I just can't believe what I used to. Why would God want me to make a difference in this world? All I do is make people sad and miserable!" Dennis tragically had misdiagnosed his own condition. Like countless others suffering from severe depression, Dennis had lost faith in himself and his ability to help others in need. In his opinion, he was nothing but a failure to everyone he wished to serve. Having neither the energy nor the courage to take on life, it would be much easier to simply give up.

It's not surprising that if the one who is depressed is apt to misdiagnose his state, so also will many people who observe his changed disposition.

So it was with Dennis' family. Time and again their conversation with him left them feeling both helpless and frustrated. "Just believe!" they told him. "With God all things are possible!" But no matter how they encouraged him, it was like talking to a wall. He was adamant that there was no chance his situation would improve or his struggles would subside. The family later learned that Dennis was unable to just believe. It simply was not possible for him to believe that he or anyone else could effect a change that would make a meaningful difference in his life.

Was Dennis lacking faith in Christ? Imagine for a moment that in your opinion your appearance is extremely unsightly to others. You believe, in fact, that you can be accurately described as "hideous in the sight of other people." If someone tells you to simply believe that God can change the fact that you are unattractive and loathsome to others, would you take that person's advice? I would guess not. You are not going to believe something about yourself that you are convinced is impossible. Like any other rational believer, you are going to conclude, "It is not a question of whether God *can* change how I am perceived by others. Indeed, with God all things are possible (Matthew 19:26), and he has the power to achieve every purpose he designs. But *will* God do what he has given me no reason to believe he will do?" There comes a point for every believer, regardless of whether he is thinking rationally, when he must simply trust in God's will.

Adding on to faith can only deprive Christians of the assurance they seek, that a suicide is with his Savior. For that reason we take comfort in knowing the truth about Christian faith. Faith may aid your self-esteem, but it is not dependent on it. Faith is dependent on your knowledge of Christ, who gives you his forgiveness. By faith you realize that God accepts you as his own, even with your sin. By faith you accept your identity as God's child through the sacrifice of his only Son. By faith you acknowledge that God has placed you into one or more specific vocations where he promises to use you in order to serve others. Despite your sin, you are God's instruments for serving others in the family, at work, and in the church! However, faith is not the same thing as self-worth or self-esteem. True faith does not believe in oneself or have faith in one's faith. It believes in Christ. It has faith in one's Savior and therefore focuses always on what is outside of self. True faith beholds the Lamb of God (John 1:29), whose sacrifice atoned for the world's sin. It looks at the work of Christ. Correspondingly, a Christian is not saved because by faith he perceives what others perceive or even what God perceives, that he is loved despite his sin. A Christian is saved because he holds by faith God's gift of forgiveness and eternal life.

That is what you may say to Dennis' family in the end. Dennis was a Christian. Perhaps he lost sight of his own path through life, but he never lost sight of the way of the cross. Even as the most despicable failure, Dennis was able to believe in Christ, who traveled to Calvary in order to redeem him.

Notes

[1]Possible synonyms for the word *self-esteem* are *self-respect* and *self-love.*

[2]Joanna McGrath and Alister McGrath, *Self-Esteem: The Cross and Christian Confidence* (Wheaton, IL: Crossway Books, A Division of Good News Publishers, 2002), p. 36.

[3]Don Matzat, *Christ-Esteem* (Eugene, OR: Harvest House Publishers, 1990), p. 43.

[4]Ibid., p. 72.

[5]Ibid., pp. 92,93.

Chapter 6

FAITH PLUS OPTIMISM

"Faith is being *sure of what we hope for* and certain of what we do not see" (Hebrews 11:1). Yet this Christian despaired, giving up on God's blessings.

Grace's mother has phoned you, requesting that you stop by the house. Her mother has become quite troubled because of several statements Grace has made recently. She's been asking what the point is in waking up in the morning. Things will never improve. She wants out. Life just hurts too much. You inquire what might cause her to say such things. Grace's mother answers, explaining that her daughter has been suffering from depression. She has been taking an antidepressant now for a few weeks. Her disturbing conversation, however, may have to do with a number of things that have changed during the last year and have caused the family a lot of grief. Her husband was forced to sell the family printing business on account of the faltering economy. For a time Grace went back to work. Shortly thereafter, however, their young son was diagnosed as having severe autism. Her mother comments, "She used to handle whatever life threw at her and with little difficulty. As of late, she's appears extremely pessimistic about everything."

Later when you arrive at Grace's home, you attempt to get her to open up and tell you what's wrong. She is unwilling to cooperate. An expression of discouragement is all you get out of her, as she cannot bring herself to look at you. After what seems like several minutes of awkward silence, Grace asserts, "Nothing is going to work out!" You answer, "Grace, you know that isn't so. God loves you!" This time there is no delay in responding to your words: "That's what you say. I happen to know God wants nothing more to do with me. He hates me!" She repeats what she voiced earlier to her mother. "I want out! God is never going to help me. I might as well die. It can't hurt as much as living!"

That was last week. Today Grace has died, having finally found a way to make the hurt go away. What will you say to her husband and mother?

63

It may serve as the most troubling evidence of suicide's paradox. A given believer gives up on God. What he was taught and accepted wholeheartedly has no seeming relevance in the last hour. This person whom others knew as a Christian loses all hope that God will come through and finally offer his help. Once again people try to resolve the paradox by embracing an aspect of natural theology and redefine faith. Those professing to be Christians will add on to what Scripture has to say about this gift by which God justifies the sinner. A final add-on to faith is optimism. With no consideration to church doctrine, we may define *optimism* as "having a positive and cheerful perspective regarding one's future." Christians expect Christians to have an optimistic attitude toward life, an attitude based on hope. A believer will hope, even expect, that good will triumph over evil. Hence, suicide's great paradox is resolved when we conclude that this person was not a believer at the time of his suicide. He exchanged his Christian optimism for a temperament marked by pessimism and gave up the faith.

Faith, however, is not the same thing as hope or maintaining an optimistic view of life. The loss of faith may lead to the loss of hope. However, the loss of hope does not always indicate a loss of faith. The loss of hope may merely suggest that a believer is experiencing extreme distress, which may be of a psychological or a physical nature. A true Christian may, in fact, lose all hope that he will regain his once comfortable tranquil life. Such a Christian may nevertheless trust in Christ for mercy and rescue from sin.

A Christian's Sense of Hopelessness

We can demonstrate the difference between faith and hope by making mention of the Christian who is mentally healthy. All believers let go of hope insofar as they worry. You worry because you are a sinner who would prefer to solve your own troubles rather than to rely on God, who provides in every circumstance. But you typically will not worry about a particular matter for hours or days at a time. You are able to separate yourself from a given solution. You know you are not the only answer. Furthermore, in time you see things improve. The severely depressed, however, often fail to disassociate themselves from the solution no matter how hard they try. The future is quite plain to them. They can fix neither their own lives nor the lives of others. Since this has become so painfully obvious to them, they lose hope. They are convinced that things will never get better and somehow they are to blame.

The Christian with major depression may obsess over the fact that he cannot turn back the clock. There is no power on earth that can alter what is or what is yet to come. Imagine yourself in a canoe with a friend. You both have lost your paddles attempting to steer your way through some rapids. Suddenly you observe that you are about to plunge over a huge waterfall. There is literally no hope that you will *not* go over the edge and that the canoe will *not* hit the bottom of the falls with tremendous velocity. If in the few moments you have left, your partner in the canoe offers a desperate prayer, you are not necessarily going to believe that events will change and you'll survive the fall. When you, in like manner, offer words of encouragement to the clinically depressed, you will not necessarily alter their perception of things. You may tell them things are sure to improve soon. Circumstances will get better, despite their assessment of things. Their depression will subside. But for the person you are hoping to lift up, no words can change what they foresee. The future is already written.

What does it mean to "hope" as a Christian?

What may prove the most difficult for you with respect to Grace's hopelessness was her conviction that God would never relieve her depression. Regardless of what we read in Hebrews 11:1, that we can be sure of what we hope for and certain of what we do not see, Grace was not sure *she would get better. She was* not certain *she would retrieve life's given joys and pleasures.*

A "depressed Christian" is not a contradiction in terms. A Christian may experience hopelessness and simultaneously trust in Christ as his sole Savior. Before proceeding, however, you should be aware that your normal usage of the word *hope* might differ from the Bible's usage of the word. Correspondingly, *losing hope* can have more than one meaning, depending on what definition of the word *hope* you use.

Natural hope

Natural hope is the term I would use for the hope we have with respect to this life and what it may hold. In the broad use of the word, you might define natural hope as the expectation that things will go well for you if not this next day, presumably in the near future. You may comment, for example, "I hope to feel better soon" or "I hope to find a new job this week." In either case, you speak of the natural hope you have concerning your day-to-day living. Such hope we call *natural* since it is natural to one's existence. This hope is as natural to one's life as one's knowledge that there is a God. It is not that hope which we obtained by the Holy Spirit when we were called to faith. It is ours simply by virtue of the fact that we are human beings created and sustained by God. We have hope because of the Son who sustains all things by his powerful Word (Hebrews 1:3).

Christian hope

The hope to which the apostles refer in New Testament Scripture we may term *Christian hope*. Christian hope is not optimism. It is a trusting anticipation or an attitude of Christian confidence. You are confident that God, in conformity with his will, will supply your needs both in this life and in the life to come (1 Corinthians 15:19-21). You have no doubt that God will give you what is best for this life, as you look forward with absolute certainty to the blessings of the next life. Christian hope is therefore free of anxiety (2 Corinthians 1:8-10). It anticipates that despite life's troubles, the day is coming when your difficulties will be removed, if not today or tomorrow at some time in the future (1 Peter 1:3). Christian hope, moreover, extends beyond the present life, helping you to overcome the fear of death. Over against seeing, Christian hope chooses to wait patiently (Romans 8:25). It yearns for relief but does not meanwhile demand answers concerning "Why this?" and "Why that?" It waits with perseverance (Romans 5:4). You can have such hope—despite the fact that you do not always get what you want—that God is faithful (Hebrews 10:23). In brief, Christian hope might be described as a day-by-day confidence in God's promise to care for you in time and in eternity however he chooses.

One possible understanding of Christian hope is this: "Regardless of how desperate I am feeling this day, in the end, God will save me." As such it finds its basis in the gospel. It is rooted in God's love and the relationship he chose to have with sinful human beings. You have hope because the Son of God became a human being in order to live and die in your place. This hope you may rest assured is *not* affected by mental illness or disruptions to your life. The only exception would occur should the believer blame God for his depression or other escalating hardships. As a rule, however, Christian hope is not affected by life-altering afflictions, since this hope is not based on what is material or tangible. It is based on the promises of God's Word. Your hope is in God and his grace. Christian hope is a gift from God, which is yours by faith. As a result, you remain convinced that God will allow nothing outside of his gracious will to upset your life. Even the hairs of your head are all numbered, Jesus declares (Matthew 10:30).

66

Christians who lose hope

When you distinguish between natural hope and Christian hope, it becomes clear that Christians on occasion do lose hope. They lose hope that they will receive relief in this life, that the Lord will help them in the same manner that he has in the past. Consider Job and his afflictions. First he lost almost all that was dear to him—all of his livestock, all of his children, and all but three of his servants (Job 1:13-19). Later, he was covered with painful sores from the soles of his feet to the top of his head (Job 2:7). Job uttered in the midst of his despair, "What strength do I have, that I should still hope?" (Job 6:11) and "I prefer strangling and death, rather than this body of mine. I despise my life; I would not live forever. Let me alone; my days have no meaning" (Job 7:15,16). Job despised his life, not his God or the grace of his God. The natural hope that had once enabled him to deal with each day as it came had deserted him.

The Question Concerning Despair

The verb *despair* may be defined as "to lose all hope" or "to be overcome by a sense of uselessness." As a noun the word is defined as "a complete loss of hope," "hopelessness," or "the feeling that everything is wrong and nothing will turn out well." In regard to people suffering from a depressive illness, I have chosen to define the verb *despair* as "to lose hope that one's situation will ever improve." There is more to it than reaching the conclusion that it is time to give up. Despair involves a yearning for relief but knowing it will never come. You and I may call this irrational. For despairing people, however, these are the facts. Despite the efforts of the most caring and professional people they could meet, they will not see any meaningful improvement.

Can a Christian despair?

In the church, despair has often been associated with suicide. To despair has been understood as giving up on God and falling from grace. Unlike other sins, despair has traditionally been the one sin that cannot be forgiven. It is believed that despair is a person's conviction that God will damn him despite what Christ has done for every sinner and therefore for him. Despair is thus a rejection of what our Savior has promised everyone on earth. By such a definition, despair is an absolute denial of God's unending willingness and capacity to forgive. The *Catholic Encyclopedia* defines *despair* as "the voluntary and complete abandonment of all hope of saving one's soul and of having the means required for that end."[1] Likewise, it is a deliberate act of the will by which a person gives up any expectation of reaching heaven.[2] As such, despair is a mortal sin, since it has determined that God has no desire to supply you with what you need to be saved.[3]

The source I have cited above distinguishes *despair* from *anxiety,* another condition of the soul, and from a sinking of the heart or overwhelming dread. I would instead propose that there are various forms of despair and that not all despairing relates to unbelief or a denial of Christ's atoning sacrifice for sinners. The teaching, however, that despair is unforgivable, has withstood the test of several centuries. It was in the fifth century when Augustine helped brand despair as a mortal sin. Since that time, church theologians have continued to discourse over the term but have fallen short in offering an adequate understanding of the word.

It ought to be evident to every pastor and teacher of the faith in the twenty-first century that not everyone who despairs, despairs of God's forgiveness. The word *despair* ought to be defined in various ways, inasmuch as it is used in various ways. The psychologist, for example, may describe a person who is despairing of life, relating that patient's hopelessness to a chemical imbalance in the bloodstream. Due to a loss of self-worth, the patient believes the people around him will be better off if he is gone. He despairs because the life he once enjoyed is irretrievable and he does not have anything to live for. We may refer to his sense of hopelessness as a *life-based despair.*

For another example, we refer to someone who is quite healthy mentally. However, he has come to realize on account of his wicked ways that there is no hope that God will accept him and save him on the basis of his works. Regardless of his many sincere efforts, he fails time after time to love the Lord his God with all his heart, with all his soul, and with all his mind, and to love his neighbor as himself (Matthew 22:37,39). As he presents himself before God, he is nothing but a sinner. We may refer to his hopelessness as a *works-based despair*. This despair, as we will discuss later, is the one type of despair we may acknowledge as beneficial.

A third person hears that despite his grave sin, Christ died for him. Despite the fact that no work he performs can make up for his sins, Jesus did everything for him. This person, however, does not believe that what his Savior did is relevant in his case. There is no hope whatsoever that God will forgive him. We may refer to his hopelessness as a *grace-based despair.*

Before elaborating on the differences between these three forms of despair, we may observe what they have in common. With each type of despair, note that the person is convinced he can no longer count on what formerly gave him a reason to hope. There are no grounds for having confidence in the future. The person who is depressed and despairing of his life complains, "Look at my life! It will never be the same, and there is nothing I can do about it! Why even go on?" The person despairing of his works remarks, "I thought I could love my way to heaven. I now know better. Even my most impressive works only bring to mind that I'm a sinner through and through!" The individual despairing of God's grace declares, "I don't care what you or anyone else tells me. I don't even care what the Bible says. God will not forgive me after what I've done. I've been at this for too long!" Whatever the case, all three forms of despair share a common attribute. The individual yearns for an end but concludes there is no chance of being relieved of his hopelessness. Each type of despair may, in fact, have this yearning in common: "I want to die!"

In the end, each type of despair involves a giving up on someone or something very dear to one's existence. The person's despair involves a kind of fleeing or abandoning. One person abandons his life. Another abandons his works, that is to say, he stops relying on them. And yet another abandons God.

Works-Based Despair

To despair of one's works is essentially to accept the message of God's law. The sinner despairs of his works as having the means to save him. Before his holy and righteous God, his works are nothing but filthy rags (Isaiah 64:6). He can do nothing to justify himself. In fact, any attempt to do so will only confirm that he has already alienated himself from Christ (Galatians 5:4). All he does or can do, as far as God is concerned, is sin and falls short of his glory (Romans 3:23).

As you think back a few weeks, you recall a conversation you had with Grace on the phone. You called her because you hadn't seen her in church for a couple months. This was unprecedented behavior on her part, as she rarely missed the service on Sunday. She promptly told you that you would see her next Sunday. What struck you at the time was the sound of shame in her voice. Many other calls you made to people who missed more than a few services have had a different tone. Some of those replies were flippant or cold, as if to say, "Pastor, you really don't have to bother me with a reminder of my negligence. If I'm not there, I must have a good reason for it." But Grace, you sensed, was on the verge of tears. She also made an ambiguous comment about her inability to be the Christian she wanted to be. She had failed as a mother, as a wife, and now as a parishioner.

We all fall short in our efforts to love our neighbor as ourselves. What Grace failed to recognize, Martin Luther came to understand the hard way. Luther believed he could justify himself before God. This he had been taught by the church. In order to be saved, he must earn God's favor. But in time Luther faced a most disturbing paradox. God requires that man be perfect in every way (Matthew 5:48). However, a person is neither righteous nor becomes righteous in God's sight through his personal efforts (Ecclesiastes 7:20). Reconciling these two truths proved to be no easy task for Luther. For years he suffered from episodes of acute depression, agonizing over his works. It became so brutal at times that he once noted: "I myself was offended more than once, and brought to the very depth and abyss of despair, so that I wished I had never been created."[4] According to Luther, no one can bear the accusations of the law. The law declares that we are sinners who fall short of God's perfect standard. We can only imagine the horrifying result should the law become the last word. On another occasion, Luther remarked, "This, then, is the thunderbolt by means of which God with one blow destroys both open sinners and false saints. He allows no one to justify himself. He drives all together into terror and despair."[5]

Inasmuch as the law is supposed to drive us to despair, a works-based despair is necessary for every believer. We are *supposed* to despair before God of our ineptness to live a righteous life. "'Is not my word like fire,' declares the LORD, 'and like a hammer that breaks a rock in pieces?'" (Jeremiah 23:29). The words of David also come to mind. "The LORD is close to the brokenhearted and saves those who are crushed in spirit" (Psalm 34:18). The word *brokenhearted* literally means "to be shattered to pieces." "Crushed in spirit," moreover, denotes that which is "pulverized as dust." It is God's way. With his law, he crushes any confidence we develop in our own works. He pulverizes our sinful ego so that our only hope for salvation is outside of ourselves. But that is where the assuring words of the gospel come in. The Lord is *close* to the brokenhearted. He *saves* those who are crushed in spirit and suffer from a works-based despair. He comes to the contrite sinner who yearns for his Savior's grace and tells him, "I am here! I will not abandon you! Receive the forgiveness I obtained for you when I shed my blood for you!"

King David, we may be sure, understood what it meant to despair of his works. David had become guilty of adultery, deceit, and murder. He made arrangements to sleep with a woman named Bathsheba, having spotted her bathing. Some time later, he learned she had conceived. Having failed to trick her husband into sleeping with her and to convince him that he was the father, David had him placed in the front line of battle where he was sure to be killed. Later David took Bathsheba to be his wife. But for some time David despaired. "When I kept silent, my bones wasted away through my groaning all day long. For day and night your hand was heavy upon me; my strength was sapped as in the heat of summer. Then I acknowledged my sin to you and did not cover up my iniquity. I said, 'I will confess my transgressions to the LORD'—and you forgave the guilt of my sin" (Psalm 32:3-5). David knew his works were evil in God's sight. He felt the hammer of God's law crush his spirit, stripping him of every ounce of human integrity. In his despair, David hoped to escape his sinful deeds. But there was nowhere to flee until he heard the absolution of Nathan: "The LORD has taken away your sin" (2 Samuel 12:13), and believed it.

Grace-based despair

A sinner who despairs of his works may in every case flee to God's grace. Regrettably, not everyone who endures the crushing blow of God's law is receptive to the gospel with its message of forgiveness. A person suffers a grace-based despair when for whatever reason he is not willing to believe he can be forgiven. Perhaps he is convinced God's law is the final word. By nature he is a sinner. As such, he stands condemned before God. There is not any use in even hoping that God would have anything else to say on the matter. Or perhaps he is of the opinion that the gospel is not absolute, that there are certain sins God will not forgive, or that God will not forgive those who have persisted in a given sin for an extended period.

Grace's mother often attempted to encourage Grace when she was suffering from the worst of her depression. "It will be a matter of time and your medicine will help you feel much better. Just give it a chance to work." But Grace did not believe she could hold on for whatever number of weeks it would take for her medication to take effect. In time she did not believe she would ever improve. There was no hope she would recover on this side of heaven. So she despaired and took the necessary steps to end her life. Did she despair of God's grace? Grace was ill, suffering from an unyielding case

71

of depression. She never abandoned her faith in Christ. She believed he would remain her Savior both in life and in death.

Inasmuch as Christ died for every sinner, grace-based despair is neither reasonable nor inevitable in anyone's case. Despair of this nature is always a consequence of temptation. Tempted by the devil, the world, or your own sinful nature, you make a personal judgment that God cannot or will not forgive you. Satan in particular is interested in spurring a grace-based despair. As had happened in Luther's case, it is the devil's desire that you perceive a paradox. You should note a contradiction when you hear what God promises on the one hand and what you must conclude on the basis of your sin on the other hand. "God may promise what he will. But how can a God who is absolutely just also be merciful? How can God, who requires that I be completely holy, forgive me when I keep sinning against him?" If the paradox remains unresolved and you deduce that God cannot forgive you, this leads to despair. To effect this outcome Satan attempts to conceal the gospel from you or to convince you that the gospel is merely theoretical. When he achieves his goal, you begin to understand forgiveness in view of what *you do* rather than in view of what *Christ has done* for you.

Grace-based despair also happens in the church when professing Christians are instructed wrongly. The law is promoted as the message that saves instead of the gospel. Instead of being taught that Christ's forgiveness is received by faith, you are told that forgiveness is obtained when you display the right behavior. You are taught that forgiveness is for those who generate the proper measure of love or remorse on account of their sins. Or you are informed that forgiveness corresponds to your inner wrestling or heartfelt vows.

In addition to generating hypocrisy in some, such teachings are sure to produce despair in others. The honest person who acknowledges his sinful nature concludes that he is incapable of following through. He cannot do what he has promised to do, and therefore he cannot be forgiven! This is the ultimate fruit of all false doctrine. People become either presumptuous hypocrites or despairing fools. Either they assume they can make themselves right in God's eyes despite their utter sinfulness or they assume that such forgiveness is *impossible* to obtain.

This explains why the church traditionally has had an easier time judging in the wake of a suicide than exercising compassion and understanding. People note the connection between suicide and despair and presume that the person who committed suicide was battling a grace-based despair. Coming to mind is the disciple Judas. For centuries he has served as the leading example of one who despaired of God's grace. What was it about Judas and his actions, that the Christian world should view as so tragic that Jesus himself should exclaim, "It would be better for him if he had not been born" (Matthew 26:24)? The Lord was not making reference to his suicide, as tragic as it was. Moreover, it was not his betrayal that generated Jesus' comment. All the disciples betrayed Christ (Matthew 26:56). Judas was different because he did not trust in God's grace for assurance that he was forgiven. Having despaired of the Lord's grace, he died in unbelief!

Even so, for centuries the church has drawn unsuitable conclusions about Christians who commit suicide and the despair they exhibit. Much of it has to do with reading things into this Judas account. The popular thinking is, If one of Christ's own disciples despaired of God's grace in the last hour and consequently ended his life, so it must be with Christians today who commit suicide. It is assumed that in any given case, suicide occurs because things got rough. "This believer gave up on Jesus and his grace." There is a big difference, though, between Judas and the typical Christian suffering from depression or hopelessness. Moreover, there is a big difference between the despair exhibited by Judas and that exhibited in the life of your average despairing Christian. Judas despaired because he became acutely aware of his wickedness. He betrayed the Son of God, his only Savior. The Christian suffering from a depressive illness, on the other hand, despairs on account of a mind-altering illness. Judas despaired because he refused to believe in the forgiveness of sins. The depressed Christian despairs in many cases because he is incapable of believing that his life is salvageable.

Life-based despair

Despair as referenced earlier may be defined as hopelessness. The hopeless individual sees his future as plugged. In his despair, he assumes change is impossible. With respect to the third form of despair, *life-based* despair, a person loses hope in God's providential care. He despairs of life's joys and blessings. He becomes convinced that his life is void of purpose and pleasure and there is no chance things will improve. The individual suffering from a type of depressive illness may despair of himself or his worth, imagining he is a worthless zero. In the end, his life is happening on a downhill slope, as it were, and he has no means of retrieving it.

Visiting with Grace's mother following the funeral, you learned a little more about her daughter's pain. Grace was unable to cover the bases as she once did as a mother and wife. She could not go back to work and at the same time be the proper mother to her young son. The solution may have seemed simple enough. Grace needed some special help. Their health insurance would help cover the cost of hiring respite workers to help their child. In addition, Grace's sister was very qualified to help care for him. She could help reduce the family expenses and the burdens that go with being a primary caregiver while holding a full-time job. However, Grace would consider neither of these options, maintaining she was the mother. It was unfortunately a short time later that she determined she could not keep up with two full-time vocations. She took this very personally and eventually despaired of the fact that she could not manage.

If you suffer from a life-based despair, it will correspond to the fact that you, for whatever reason, are lacking in *natural* hope as we have defined the term. This may occur if, due to depression, you perceive that you are no longer of any value to the people you have loved, and you withdraw from them. Or it may happen should something happen to one or many of the relationships you have developed. Similarly, you may despair of your life if you are suddenly handicapped or suffer a major financial setback. You determine, in any event, that you are no longer capable of serving people or enjoying life.

All people are vulnerable to experiencing a life-based despair at some point in their lives. This is because everyone is conceived in sin. You someday may find yourself lacking in natural hope. Even if only temporarily, you may experience hopelessness if the life you have come to love and cherish has been suddenly lost and you are convinced it will never be retrieved. If you despair of your life under such circumstances, fellow Christians will not infer that you have also despaired of God's grace. You have lost hope—not *Christian* hope but *natural* hope. Your natural knowledge of God is no longer informing you that his blessings will sustain your life. Natural hope ordinarily is cut off by the prospect of imminent death as when one is dying of cancer. It also occurs, unfortunately, when—due to mental illnesses or extreme circumstances—one *perceives* that one's life is already over for all practical purposes.

The Church's Understanding of Despair

Many in the church today, I am afraid, have one definition for the word *despair*. It comes closest to resembling a grace-based despair.

Why they have taken this unfortunate position, I suspect is because they either lack an understanding of the gospel or they are ignorant regarding mental illness and depression. In any event, they have drawn unfortunate conclusions about the faith of someone who is ill and despairs of his life. They assume that the person who loses hope in God's daily care also loses hope in God's grace.

There is a much more suitable explanation of course. Faith in Christ is inseparably linked to Christian hope, not natural hope. In the daily struggle against temptation, a Christian may lose confidence in God's providential care, but never in God's grace. He may conclude that nothing will ever go right for him in this life while believing at the very same time that he is forgiven through the blood of Christ. The same may hold true for you someday. Overwhelmed by life's changes, you may note that you are absolutely perplexed with respect to God's *temporal* blessings, but not to the point where you despair with respect to God's *eternal* blessings (2 Corinthians 4:8). You still believe. Remember, faith does not save because it trusts in God's ability to provide in the worst of circumstances. Faith saves because it possesses the forgiveness of sins obtained for us by Christ.

Once the church comes to understand despair in an appropriate way, Christians will adopt a proper view of suicide. It is my hope that instead of bringing to mind Judas, who despaired of God's grace, a suicide will bring to mind a biblical figure who simply lost hope in life. Coming to mind may be Samson. True, his death is not normally viewed as a suicide but as a sacrifice. The thoughts of Samson prior to his death, however, may be more indicative of what happens for many believers who desire to end their lives. Samson suffered from a life-based despair. Having revealed the secret of his strength to God's enemies, he was overcome by the Philistines, who gouged out his eyes and made sport of his weakened condition. He felt he had forsaken God and betrayed his people. He was a loser who had no further purpose in life other than to kill himself in order to score a major victory against God's enemies. In similar fashion, today's believer who finds the means to end his life, in more cases than not, has suffered a despair that relates to shame and defeat. Oftentimes he wants to die because he sees this as a better outcome for those whom he loves. It would be inappropriate to conclude that he despaired of God grace and therefore fell away from the faith.

The despairing Christian

Despair does not always have a spiritual orientation. Its basis often is strictly psychological. The loss of hope has to do with a medical condition. Something gets out of whack from a chemical stand-point and how messages are being carried between various neurons in the brain. The depressed person is not capable of reorienting his thoughts. He obsesses on what is wrong in his life and despairs. For this reason, the question whether a Christian can despair may be best answered by spending some time explaining how we can and ought to distinguish between despair as a medical condition and despair as a spiritual condition. The first despair is related to genet-ics and how one may be predisposed to mental illness, depression, and related psychological effects. The second despair is linked to a rejection of the gospel. One has to do with a horrendous physical affliction; the other, with unbelief.

This isn't to say that despair will never take on a spiritual conno-tation for the Christian. Every believer at times suffers from a works-based despair. He experiences hopelessness because he has fallen short in his effort to love God and his neighbor. Having sinned he feels sorrow. But then he hears and trusts in the gospel. He believes Christ has taken his sin away. For the person suffering from a clinical depression, a different story is told. Christ's forgive-ness may be declared and re-declared. Nevertheless, he finds no relief from his despair and *will* not without a chemical correction or a change in medication.

There is something, meanwhile, that may complicate matters if you desire to minister to the despairing individual. The depressed person may fail to distinguish between a works-based despair and a life-based despair. Instead of recognizing that his depression is affect-ing certain thoughts of his, he believes he is experiencing hopeless-ness because of who he is or what he has done. Consequently, having misdiagnosed his despair, he relys on the wrong kind of treatment. Instead of seeking relief through the gospel, to say nothing about his doctor, he listens to his illness, which prescribes no remedy to his grief but persists in its accusations and condemnations.

The pastor's prognosis

Most people it may seem will know better. God does not drive a person to despair on the basis of what this person *perceives* to be sin-ful. God prompts us to despair on the basis of what he *reveals* to be sinful in his law. And after one acknowledges his sin, he can believe his sin is gone from God's sight. "If we confess our sins, he is faithful and just and will forgive us our sins and purify us from all unright-eousness" (1 John 1:9).

There is a temptation, nevertheless, that faces today's pastor. You maintain that depression is in *every case* a sign of an inward ongoing spiritual battle. A paradox is observed. You know that a Christian trusts in God and the Lord's blessings by which he sustains all life. Yet this person you knew as a Christian despaired. He gave up on God and his blessings. That is why he took his life! In an attempt to resolve the paradox, you determine that the *act of despair* is the same as losing one's faith.

Even if you choose to be more informed on this subject than some, it may be next to impossible to comprehend what it means to become suicidal in one's thinking and to despair. "How can a Christian get to this point?" you may ask. If you have trouble identifying with someone who has lost the will to live, understand that such a Christian is not ordinarily despairing of God's *grace*. He is despairing of his *life*. It is not that he lacks faith in Christ and his promises concerning eternal life. Suffering from a severe form of depression or another depressive illness, he lacks hope that his current personal situation will ever improve or that God will help him.

It is not easy to determine what is behind an individual's despair. This is so because an individual who is not thinking in a normal fashion may himself mistake one kind of despair for another. Keep in mind that an individual may do his despairing based on misinformation resulting from irrational thinking. One person despairs of his works, imagining that he has committed some grievous sin. And he has done no such thing. He has conjured up the whole thing in his head. Another person despairs of his life, imagining his life is in a state that is beyond repair. But his delusional thinking has concocted the whole thing. The only thing that needs fixing is his medication. Still another despairs of God's grace (so it would seem), imagining that the Lord's grace cannot possibly apply to his situation. But once again he is mistaken. The Lord does not want "anyone to perish, but everyone to come to repentance" (2 Peter 3:9). In each case, the despair is caused by his illness rather than a legitimate evaluation of the facts. This point is essential to take into account, since in the third case we are speaking of a *false* despair. It therefore has no bearing on his salvation. He despairs not because he has truly abandoned Christ and his forgiveness. Rather, *he* is the one who has been abandoned by his own thoughts, due to his sickness.

Faith in the proper light

In what context may we speak of the faith of a suicide? If one adds to what faith is and how it saves, the ambiguity remains as to whether you can say a suicide is in heaven. As a result, you do not alleviate the pain and the grief experienced by the survivors. The severely depressed and despairing person will be judged and stigmatized as one who should be stripped of the title "Christian."

Unfortunately, from the time Christ's church was first established, theologians and laity alike have tried to add to what Christ has said regarding faith. They have consulted human reason instead of Scripture and have embraced natural theology instead of relying on a theology based on the Bible's teaching on sin and grace. True Christian faith does not consist of the believer's works of obedience or what a Christian does because he is a Christian. Nor is Christian faith a faith in one's ability to reason or faith in one's concept of self. Nor is it faith in one's life. Faith is trust in Christ and his gift of forgiveness. That is why faith saves, because it clings to the gospel and receives the forgiveness Christ earned for us. By God's gift of faith, we become righteous in the sight of God.

Understanding what you do about Christian faith, you may assure Grace's husband and mother that she is in heaven. Yes, she despaired of her life. But she did not despair of God's grace. She never gave up on Christ. Tell them she was a Christian, because the loss of hope does not constitute the loss of faith. Grace may not have beaten her illness, but through the Word and the sacraments, she did beat sin, death, and the devil. "For everyone born of God overcomes the world. This is the victory that has overcome the world, even our faith" (1 John 5:4).

Notes

[1]The *Catholic Encyclopedia,* Volume 4 (New York: Robert Appleton Company, 1908), http://www.newadvent.org (accessed January 15, 2007).

[2]Ibid.

[3]Ibid.

[4]*Luther's Works,* p. 190.

[5]Smalcald Articles III, III:2-7, Tappert, *The Book of Concord,* p. 304.

Part Three

Suicide From a Perspective
of Sin and Grace

Chapter 7

ATTAINING AN UNDERSTANDING

We saw in part 2 that the stigma relating to a Christian's suicide corresponds to various false doctrines regarding Christian faith. Instead of resolving suicide's paradox, insinuations are made that the suicide had a deficient faith. Unfair judgments about the deceased Christian are made furthermore when clergy lack workable definitions of *sin* and *grace*. People presume that God's grace covers only certain kinds of sins and that the sin of suicide will inevitably escort a person away from his grace.

Naturally, labeling someone as weak or sick will not provide an acceptable explanation of the person's suicide. So that you might obtain a satisfactory understanding of this matter, you must take an adequate look at the suicide. You must ask why he wished to end his life despite what he believed about his Savior. What was he thinking?

A Sense of Hopelessness—Suicide's Common Denominator

By nature human beings believe that life is worth living, even with life's adversities. Yet this person lost all hope that his life had value.

Notice that the focus of our paradox has changed, as it has to do not with being a believer per se but with being human. It may serve nevertheless as the most difficult paradox to resolve in a suitable fashion. If you have not been suicidal and lost the will to continue, how do you relate to someone who has? How can you possibly understand him in his miseries? If, in your opinion, life is good since life is from God, you, quite frankly, may be incapable of conceiving the thought that life is not worth living.

Is there a single reason why most suicides take place?

Most experts who are asked this question will say that there is not a sole cause of suicide. It can be next to impossible, in fact, to determine in a particular case the reason or reasons why the person chose to end his life. You may compare a given suicide with an air disaster.

Following an unexplained tragedy in the air, investigators will typically perform a very thorough search for the "black box." The thinking is that we must know what went wrong! And after determining what went awry, we must take the proper steps to see that this never happens again. The black box will provide the answers we are looking for. Unfortunately, under many such circumstances, complete answers are never found.

A similar scenario is drawn when someone commits suicide. What happened? Was he troubled? How? Why? Was he seriously ill or was there some recent catastrophic incident in his life that triggered this event? Was it a combination of factors, some being of a biological nature, some having a genetic or environmental basis? Biological factors may include such things as heredity, pregnancy, menstruation, psychoses, and diabetes. People have also attributed the act of suicide to many and various motives or environmental causes: bravery and cowardice, patriotism, wisdom, fear, pride, envy, loneliness, alcoholism, a desire to punish oneself or another. Some are said to have taken their lives because they wanted vengeance or a way of exercising emotional blackmail. Some are described as glory seekers who want to execute power or control. Others wish to be reunited with a loved one. Various researchers attribute suicides to seasonal and economic fluctuations, some even seeing a correlation between suicidal deaths and atmospheric pressure and sunspots.[1]

According to most authorities on the subject of suicide, there is almost never one reason for which a given suicide takes place. We may argue, rather, that nearly every suicide is the product of a variety of factors which together manage to interact in a fatal mix.[2] Some suicidologists insist that an exploration of suicide must be three-dimensional, examining the problem psychologically, biologically, and sociologically.[3]

Irrespective of the many cited causes of suicide, it is my belief that there is one feature which all suicides share—a crushing sense of hopelessness. Excluding as a possibility, perhaps, involuntary drug overdose or the case of a suicide not understanding the consequences of his action, the lack of hope is suicide's common denominator. The suicidal person is fixated on the present. The future provides no hope from his standpoint, and this causes him to dwell on what appears to be wrong here and now. In time his fixation becomes an obsession that feeds on itself, since he cannot fix his current problems. And this only adds to his sense of hopelessness. David D. Burns comments in this regard: "The critical decision to commit suicide results from your illogical conviction that your mood can't improve. You feel certain that the future holds only more pain and turmoil! . . . Like some depressed patients, you may be able to support your pessimistic prediction with a wealth of data which seems to you to be overwhelmingly convincing."[4] Naturally, it usually takes a while to convince yourself of something so dreadful. Even so, every suicide results from the person's seeking relief from his hopelessness.

Useful study of suicide may be confined to four major categories, the first two relating to mental illness. Most frequently, we will analyze a suicide based on whether the deceased had some history with depression. A mental disorder or psychological factor may have also been involved. In addition, it is possible that he was wrestling with an increasing number of stresses, which in time had an accumulative effect on him. A final possibility is that the suicide had recently encountered a traumatic event, which in his opinion had absolutely devastated his life. Furthermore, a given suicide may be characterized by a combination of the above, which have somehow worked together. The individual determines, whether gradually or very suddenly, that all is hopeless, that life holds nothing remotely good for him or beneficial for others.

1. Depression

Depression is a mental illness that alters a person's perception of himself and the life he is currently living. It commonly features anxiety and shame, guilt and anger, intense sadness and difficulty concentrating, as well as a sense of hopelessness, worthlessness, and helplessness. About 90 percent of suicides are related to depression, other mood disorders, or substance abuse disorders, which are often combined with mental disorders.[5]

The individual who has not been diagnosed properly may not be aware that he is severely depressed. All he knows is that he's ashamed of the way he feels and believes he ought to be able to "suck it up" and get on with life. But he does not. Instead, he is consumed by those things over which he has no control and often blames himself for everything that seems off-kilter in life. Should he want to talk about the way he is feeling, oftentimes he will not. He feels too ashamed. Frequently the nature of severe depression is such that the person does not wish to reveal what he is thinking.

The worst part of major depression may be the inability to shake the belief that your pain will continue for the rest of your life. The problem is that you can trace your depression back to your own deficiencies, which you believe are insurmountable. When the verdict is finally in, you can't stand being in the same room with yourself. But how do you get away from yourself?

2. Other psychological factors

Like depression, other psychological factors may eat away at a sense of hope that life will return to any kind of normalcy. Again, the suicide is convinced that he will never be relieved of the anguish that plagues him internally on a perpetual basis. About 15 percent of individuals diagnosed with mood disorders such as severe depression and bipolarity, or with psychotic disorders such as schizophrenia, or with substance abuse attempt to kill themselves.[6]

3. Accumulative stresses

Accumulative stresses can also take a substantial toll on an individual's assessment of his future and whether he foresees anything but doom and gloom. This consists, to a great extent, of severe changes in a person's life or the constant struggle to adjust to change or to multiple roles. Although these stresses may build in the person very gradually, the cumulative effect can be just as devastating as depression or other psychological illnesses and disorders. Such stresses are often environmental in nature and therefore may fester for some time undetected and untreated.

4. Traumatic event

A final category to be considered in our study of suicide is the "traumatic event." This consists of a single painful incident in life, which generates an instant sense of hopelessness. An example may be the end of a relationship, such as a divorce or the death of someone close. It may also consist of the loss of a job, a major change in health, or some other event that proves to be traumatic or extremely painful.

Less than 5 percent of all suicides result from what has been labeled by some as "impulsive panic behavior."[7] I believe traumatic events, nevertheless, are relevant to our discussion. More than just a few suicides, after all, will occur among those who suffer from a combination of depression, other psychological problems, and accumulative stresses. It can often be the traumatic event that serves as a catalyst provoking a person to self-destructive behavior. By itself, the traumatic event will not result in suicide as frequently as the other three categories I have outlined. Traumatic changes in a person's life, however, may precipitate a depressive illness if he is predisposed to such an illness.

In a few words, let me comment on five different suicides, each marked by a sense of hopelessness. (The following people represent real individuals with whom the author was acquainted who died by suicide. With the exception of the aforementioned, Jean, the details pertaining to the loss of hope and the suicides' eventual deaths have been changed.) Serving as an example under both the first and second categories, I will refer to my wife, Jean.

1. *Jean* (depression)

Jean was suffering from major depression, also known as clinical depression. The illness had robbed her of her perception that life had any redeeming qualities. Despite the fact that she was extremely creative and caring and had a very happy disposition, her wonderful world would in time become a hopeless monstrosity. Every joy she had known in life was, as far as she was concerned, lost—never again to be retrieved. All she felt was intense shame, which could be traced back to the worthless person she believed she had become.

Jean's illness was the main element behind her sense of hopelessness. When she was first diagnosed with clinical depression, I believe she truly was looking forward to getting better. She hoped her medication would make a difference, and she had reason to believe it would. Her psychiatrist was confident that it was just a matter of time before she would be feeling much better. Moreover, for a time she enjoyed an appreciable improvement. Although she had given up both directing the church choir and tending to her homeschooling responsibilities, she was hoping to serve the church again on Sunday mornings by playing the organ and singing an occasional solo and by volunteering as a substitute teacher at a neighboring Lutheran elementary school. But her ambitions proved to be nothing more than short-lived fantasies. Despite her new medication, she soon plunged into an extremely deep depression from which there would be no recovery. This medication was the final of three or four different prescriptions Jean had been given over the span of several months. She would try a medication, and for a while it would have some beneficial effect. But in every case it had a way of short-circuiting. It would suddenly just stop working! Thus Jean lost all hope that things would improve. In addition, she began feeling terribly guilty for becoming what she perceived to be a burden to so many. In her opinion she was a failure as a mother, as a wife, and as a musician. I found her the morning she chose to end her life in the basement with a plastic bag over her head.

2. *Jean and a prior attempt* (other psychological factors)

For several months Jean had suffered from what I would characterize as paranoid delusions. She began to read into a variety of things that were largely trivial in nature. It might be a friendly exchange she had with a parishioner, a stranger she saw in the grocery store, or even a news clip on TV or a billboard advertisement. Jean's memory for details permitted her to assemble over time more and more evidence of a conspiracy. What to me was obviously a jumble of unrelated bits of data, she would piece together as incontestable proof that people were attempting to build a case against her. It was bound to "come out" in a certain church publication, not to mention the national news, and would reflect on my family, particularly my father, whose seminary presidency would be over if the truth about her was made public.

As her condition worsened, the delusions became increasingly bizarre. She spoke concerning aliens who were trying to uncover her past. Thinking back on what she said to me, it was quite ironic. I was the one who loved watching science fiction. She hated movies about aliens and creatures from other worlds. She did not want to imagine for a moment that those extraterrestrial freaks could be real. But as Jean became more ill, she was the one whose imagination would concoct beings from another planet. Friends and family in a very systematic fashion were being replaced with look-alikes. These "clones," as they were, had a very simple objective: to alienate Jean from the rest of the world and expose her for the vile sinner she was. Allegedly, she was not worthy of life—not as a mother or teacher, not as a wife, not as a daughter or sister, daughter-in-law or sister-in-law, not as a parishioner. Eventually Jean came to suspect everyone—people at church, friends whom we had made years earlier, even me, her husband. On occasion, I was successful at talking her out of her delusions. However, even if I had been able to penetrate this wall—seemingly impervious to reason—it would not last. Ultimately, I could not compete with the voices she heard from the growing number of clones who apparently were capable of speaking to her via telepathy. Had I pressed her on what the voices were saying, I had the impression she was being told to sacrifice herself. How many times Jean had resisted giving in to the coercing voices with their orders, I cannot be sure. What I do know is that having lost hope of winning the fight, she lost the will to live. Jean's first attempt to end her life was to fire a shot from our son's BB gun into the roof of her mouth.

I will never forget the look we received from the doctor in emergency as we sat before him, calm and somber, and he asked us why we were there. It was as though he was blurting out in disbelief: "Are you sure you attempted suicide?! Where's the crisis?" What he and others, I am sure, had failed to understand that day is, this was Jean's cry for help. And as for me, I believe I was in shock.

3. **Brian** *(accumulative stresses)*

Brian was a marine who had been stationed in Iraq for 12 months. Upon returning home he soon began suffering from an extreme sense of loneliness. Prior to his deployment and the day he uttered his good-byes, he had felt like a patriot on a pedestal. Upon completing his mission, he was not the man he had aspired to be. While in Iraq he had let his fellow troops down. Under what is called buddy care, *the marines in Iraq had a system by which they would assure each other's safety and account for their whereabouts. Every marine was assigned a buddy, or aide, so that the two might serve as a means of support to each other, as well as an extra pair of eyes. Sadly, the marine assigned to Brian was killed one day by a roadside bomb. It was Brian's opinion that the care he had extended his comrade was ineffective. He had made it out okay, but his buddy had been lost.*

Back at home matters went from bad to worse. Over the span of a few weeks, he had four different jobs, but one by one he saw them fall through. It was apparent to the people hiring him that while he was back in the States, his mind was still on the war. He had trouble concentrating on his work and was described by his employers as withdrawn and depressed. They also learned that he suffered from post-traumatic stress disorder but refused to seek help, since "real marines" didn't require such assistance.

Pressure continued to build when his girlfriend of three years urged him to take appropriate steps to firm up plans for the future. She, after all, had given birth to his daughter while he was away. In her opinion, it was time to settle down. But in his view, it just wasn't possible. Living happily ever after wasn't realistic at this stage. It was very possible he would be redeployed. Therefore, any engagement had to be put on hold.

Brian and his girlfriend never did come to an agreement on their future. Shortly after she made it plain to him that she did not want to wait with marriage and would not wait, he made the decision to end his life. Brian was found lying flat on his back on his fully dressed bed in a full-length position. He was in complete uniform as though being presented for the viewing of a funeral. Tucked in a pocket by the lapel of his coat was a note. It read: "I'm so sorry, Dear! I've failed you. I've failed God and I've failed my country. Don't be sorry for me. I was unable to continue on this track.

Life's stresses became unbearable for me. Everyone's life will be happier and less burdensome if I'm no longer with you. Be strong. I know you and little Emma will be better off without me. I'm sorry! Signed: I'll love you always, Brian." Brian died of an overdose of barbiturates.[8]

4. **John** *(traumatic event)*

The suicide of John—while just as tragic in nature as the others I have cited—is different in a number of respects. He had no history of mental illness of any kind, had never been medicated for a mood disorder, and was never hospitalized for having attempted suicide. His associates had described him as one who was extremely steady and consistent in his work. He was a single man working for a financial company that had recently transferred him to New York.

His office was located in the second of the twin towers to collapse on September 11, 2001. It was on that day his life in a few short moments literally flashed before his eyes. In the brief time it took to arrive in his office, to comprehend what was happening to the neighboring tower, and to feel the massive jolt of the second airliner when it hit a few stories below him, he determined that his perfectly safe and secure life was about to end. And what could he do about it? Nothing! A most horrifying death was imminent for him and for the many others on the same floor. What is more, there was no hope of escaping the agony it promised. The circumstances as he read them offered him no other alternative. His only real choice was the mode of death. Should he trade one ending for another? Be slowly baked alive or jump? In his estimation, it truly was no choice at all. John elected not to sit and wait.

5. **Barb** *(a combination)*

Barb was a teenager who had recently been diagnosed as bi-polar and had been suffering from its effects for about a year. Despite her illness, she remained a perfectionist. She was a straight-A student and talented soloist. She had developed a system by which she was able to excel during her manic periods and relax to a certain extent during her depressive phases. In consultation with her teachers at her high school, she worked weeks ahead on assignments and even took exams early to keep her grades up.

Personal struggles began to build and fester some months after the death of her mother and the breakup with her boyfriend. They had both proved very supportive to her when her depression hit her hard and she was tempted to withdraw from family and friends. Barb's mother was her motivator when it came to her studies and encouraged her daily to achieve what she could to remain ahead. Her boyfriend, who was extremely understanding, helped her plot out her social calendar and school activities. With the two of them gone, however, Barb's life underwent some difficult transitions. On the one hand, she was spending more time at home studying and less time with friends. On the other hand, she was no longer seeing the benefits of the time and dedication invested in her education. Moreover, her father was unable to fill the void that Barb was now experiencing. As busy as he was with his work and keeping up on additional responsibilities at home, he could not find time to address his daughter's struggles.

Barb, meanwhile, had come up with her own read on matters. It was her fault that her father was not coming to her recitals. Perhaps had she been awarded that scholarship her mother had spoken about, her father would exhibit a little more attention. If only she had retained her 4.0, she would not feel compelled to talk to Dad about college finances and receiving help. For a while father-daughter conflicts were a daily affair. Where was the money to come from to pay for her schooling? They needed to talk about her future. Eventually, however, Barb gave up speaking to her father. She internalized her frustrations, reasoning that her father, upon whom she relied for her success as a young lady, simply was unable to help.

It was late one night that Barb drove off a steep cliff. Because the highway was quite curvy, people may have gotten the impression that she had taken her eyes off the road. However, the state trooper who filed the accident report found a somewhat ambiguous note in Barb's wallet. "I'm sorry!" she wrote. "I'm tired of being a disappointment and letting everyone down. You shouldn't have to deal with my hardships if I can't even deal with them. I love you. Signed: Barb."

*6. **Karl** (a combination)*

Karl had suffered from depression as a young man when he first set out on his own. As a result he had made some major adjustments in his life and mentally had been doing fine for several decades. His depression resurfaced in his mid-70s when he suffered a sudden deterioration of his health. He was being treated for severe arthritis and was dealing with persistent dizzy spells, which his doctor believed were associated with a benign tumor located in his brain. Simple tasks had in many cases become arduous and drawn out ordeals. Eventually he lost his driver's license when an untimely spell resulted in a minor accident involving another car.

Moderate depression developed quickly into hopelessness and despair when within a two-week period Karl lost his wife to a heart attack and was himself diagnosed with an aggressive cancer of the bladder. In no time he became indifferent about the days ahead. He began to eat less, drink more, and lose an interest in shopping for household necessities. He was preoccupied with a feeling of inadequacy and found every excuse for neglecting a growing number of daily obligations. His children soon confronted him with the unhealthy patterns they observed and offered to help in any way they could. Perhaps they could take over the handling of finances, which their mother had always assumed. But their gracious gestures simply reinforced his view that his life was over and that he would not overcome his sense of loss. When he did visit with his children, he complained about living out a prolonged and degrading existence from the cancer. He used to be the family member everyone turned to. He was the practical one, the one who always had the solutions. And now look at him! He was incapable of dealing with either his loss or his disability. The only thing which would mark his life in its final chapter was the feeling of immense humiliation.

Or perhaps he wasn't done acting in his family's best interest! There was one more thing he could do. It was a short time after speaking with the funeral home director, whom he made aware of his cancer, that Karl was found in the attic with his rifle resting beside him still warm from its final blast. One last time he would be the one issuing the practical decision for the family.

The Great Escape

 By nature human beings have a will to live. Yet this person developed the will to kill himself.

The cry for help: Did he really wish to die?

Yes and no. It is noteworthy that suicide attempts and suicidal "gestures" outnumber actual suicides by as many as 10 to 1. This illustrates the person's ambivalence. He may be undecided about whether to choose life or death. The attempt is a cry for help. He is hoping someone will rescue him before death occurs.[9]

You may ask, "Why go to such an extreme?" Losing complete hope and the ability to manage or alter your life is one thing. But ending your life? That's an entirely different matter! For the prospective suicide, however, it is not seen so much as a choice between life and death. All they know is something must change. For most people, life consists of making continuous choices day after day. People contemplating suicide are not *able* to make simple choices in the way most people do. Edwin Shneidman, in his work *The Suicidal Mind,* remarks: "I believe that people who are actually committing suicide are ambivalent about life and death at the very moment they are committing it. They wish to die *and* they simultaneously wish to be rescued. . . . I have never known anyone who was 100 percent for wanting to commit suicide without any fantasies of possible rescue. Individuals would be happy not to do it, if they didn't 'have to.'"[10] Many if not most people, to be sure, who attempt suicide would choose something less definite if they believed they had an alternative. For this reason some experts will speak of the "suicide gesture." The suicidal gesture, as it is, is a cry not only of distress, or a cry for help, it is a plea for help by the tormented one to find a way to live.[11]

We return our thoughts to Barb for a moment. Upon the investigation of her accident, the police discovered skid marks on the road where her car had driven off the cliff. It is possible that she was not fully committed to terminating her life. Had she no reservations whatsoever, surely she would have driven at top speed through the guardrail. That would have made her plan foolproof. It is feasible, however, that her desires were mixed. Yes, she wanted to die, but only as a means of receiving help. What she truly yearned for, however, was life.

I should point out that not everyone informed about the suicidal mind agrees with respect to the suicide's motive and whether he truly wants to be saved. One author offers this warning concerning those contemplating suicide: "It can be highly misleading to view suicidal thoughts and actions as a 'plea for help.' Many suicidal patients want help *least* of all, because they are 100 percent convinced they are hopeless and beyond help. Because of this illogical belief, what they really want is death."[12] There are a variety of opinions on what most suicides are thinking prior to putting their suicide plan into action. In the end, a particular suicide should never be lumped into some category with several other suicides. I am of the opinion that every suicide is unique. In some cases the individual may be hoping for a miracle, yearning for someone to intervene and give him some reason for living. In other cases, the only matter on his mind is his everlasting misery, as he perceives it. And that begs the question, Are you going to plead for help if you *don't believe* you can be helped?

Psychological pain: What was his objective in ending his life?

Someone who is suicidal is often ambivalent about living or dying. This may not explain to you, however, why he doesn't delay death a little longer and a little longer yet. I am not sure I can answer that. I do know that the pain endured by those who take their lives is quite possibly beyond what you and I can understand. They are convinced that they can no longer endure their escalating sense of hopelessness. I believe suicide occurs because the suicide seeks to escape from pain. He has come to believe that the hopelessness he's experiencing will never end. And for that reason it has become intolerable. Psychological pain, as one writer has put it, is the basic ingredient of suicide.[13] The same author refers to the pain as *psychache*. "Psychache is the hurt, anguish, or ache that takes hold in the mind. It is intrinsically psychological—the pain of excessively felt shame, guilt, fear, anxiety, loneliness, anger, dread of growing old or of dying badly. . . . Suicide happens when the psychache is deemed unbearable and death is actively sought to stop the unceasing flow of painful consciousness."[14]

Perhaps we would rather not be capable of comprehending such a thing as psychological pain and why it leads to suicide. Then again, it is the one context in which I am inclined to comment on Jean's mode of death. The average person who suddenly had a bag placed over his head, cutting off all oxygen to his lungs, would fight with every ounce of energy to remove the bag. Let us say you became the subject of such a sick prank. Even if the incident lasted but a few moments and was not intended to harm you in any way, you would likely use whatever strength you had to punch and scratch and bite, if just to receive a gasp of air. Even so, the very bag that you would fight with all fury to escape, Jean clung to with all her might. As far as she was concerned, you see, the bag did not represent pain. It represented deliverance. Death by suffocation did not compare to the pain of hopelessness from which she would soon be relieved.

Psychological pain, I am convinced, is a pain with which the typical individual having never experienced severe depression is not capable of comprehending. When you or I must endure a given pain or aggravation, we typically can wait until the appropriate time to receive relief. A particular suicide may be depicted as one who can no longer wait for the required relief. He simply cannot tolerate the pain for another moment. You may compare him to the mother who is being pestered by her child while attempting to speak on the phone. Some time passes and the child persists in his badgering. Tapping his mother on the waist he whines, "Mommy! Mommy! Mommy!" Then comes that unpredictable but seemingly inevitable moment. Mommy lashes out with a slap or with those regrettably harsh words: "WHAT?! LEAVE ME ALONE! GET OUT OF HERE!" Very compulsively, the mother acts, not mindful of the effect her outbursts may have on her child. She simply desires relief. So it may be for the suicide who does not necessarily want to die, but acts in a very compulsive way.

No other option

Normally, the person under severe distress is aware of a number of acceptable courses of action from which he may choose to alleviate his suffering. The suicidal, in many instances, are able to focus on only one option at any given time. A core feature of suicidal thinking, in fact, is the belief that there are only two choices in the end: pain or terminating one's consciousness.[15] It is not that this person desires death. He may not want to die any more than the hospice patient who is dying of cancer. What he believes, however, is another matter. Death in his mind is inevitable. It is a simple case of having examined the facts. His pain is unbearable, and the only way the pain is going to stop is if he kills himself. Shneidman speaks as one left with this one option: " 'There was nothing else to do.' 'The only way out was death.' 'The only thing I could do [was to kill myself,] and the only way to do it was to jump from something good and high.' . . . 'Either I achieve this specific (almost magical) happy solution *or* I cease to be.' All or nothing."[16]

The suicide of King Saul deserves mention at this point. The Israelites are engaged in intense battle against the Philistines. Saul's three sons are killed. Shortly, Saul himself is critically wounded by archers. The possibilities of how matters might end is clear. He can be abused and die by the hands of his enemies or he can die by his own hand. After his armor-bearer refuses to run his sword through his king, Saul falls on his own sword (1 Samuel 31:1-6). It was his only option as far as he was concerned. He knew he was going to die, and at least by taking matters into his own hands, he could spare himself and his people the humiliation of being overcome by their enemy. He could die an honorable death on his own terms.

As an example of the person who is convinced he has no other option, imagine being on fire and the only way to put the fire out is to put your life out. You are waiting desperately to be rescued from a tall apartment compound that has caught fire. But time is swiftly running out. As you cling to the outside of a window, you suddenly observe that your clothes have caught on fire. What are your options? Perhaps you cannot prevent your death. However, you do have the means to stop the mounting pain caused by the flames. Your one option is to jump.

Perhaps you will argue concerning the person who is suicidal. You understand that he is under incredible distress. Perhaps he has been coping with pain for some time. However, he is not on fire. You are thinking: "He's held on *this* long. What finally convinces him that he can no longer tolerate the pain?" The answer is, in time something like an alarm goes off in the person's mind. It is set off by an event or situation that acts as a catalyst of sorts, finally convincing him he has no other option. He can no longer endure the current pain. He must end it and end it now.

From our previously mentioned case studies, we refer to John, who jumped on 9/11 from one of the twin towers. Although he was not on fire when he decided to jump, he clearly believed he had no other option. The catalyst was the realization that his office was suddenly getting quite warm. He knew it would not be long before the entire floor was in flames. There was no escaping being burned alive. The only way of avoiding the most excruciating death conceivable was to choose another. Brian's catalyst was his girlfriend's decision to break off their relationship. She had said she was no longer willing to wait to get married. Either they get married before he headed back to Iraq, or she was moving on. He said no, and she called his bluff telling him good-bye. That is when things suddenly became very clear to him. He had lost her, and the prospect of spending the rest of his life without her was unbearable. Barb's catalyst was some words spoken by her father. Inasmuch as she had lost her college scholarship and he could not afford to pay for her first semester, she should give up the idea of pursuing a degree in vocal music, for the next couple years anyway. In her opinion, it was now official. She was a nobody. She had lost her mother, her boyfriend had left her, and now she was stripped of the only meaningful identity she had left, her future as a professional musician. Karl's catalyst similarly would be linked to the sudden recognition that his life had robbed him of his identity. One morning as he was going through his desk, he determined that one of his children had paid a couple bills for him and tried to balance his checkbook. At last it was plain to him the direction his life was heading. His future was nothing more than a futile and demeaning exercise at trying to be in charge, but having to settle for a worthless existence as an invalid.

In my wife's case, I believe it was the final words she heard me speak that served as suicide's catalyst. Our youngest had just returned home after staying with some friends for a number of weeks. It was morning. Jean had said she was ready to be a mother again and care for our daughter. But, as had been her custom often times for numerous months, she refused to get out of bed. Despite what she had told her friend and me, she was not up to the task and she knew it. That is when I uttered what I will always regard as the most unfortunate words of my life. "Unless you get out of bed now, you will have no other choice but to be hospitalized again."

A catalyst is what incites the suicide to implement his plan to end his life. It has occurred to him that he alone can put out the pain of hopelessness by his act of suicide. And it is suddenly evident that there is no longer anything standing in the way. Whatever has prevented or delayed his suicide act up until now is no longer a factor.

A flight to grace: Wasn't he concerned about what God might think of his suicide?

Apart from a suicide note, it can be very difficult to determine what a person might have been thinking at the time he committed suicide. One thing is clear. He yearned to be free of his pain. Hence, when he determined how he would make this so, he was not willing to consider the ramifications. If we could read his mind, I am sure we would hear something like "Get me off this slide to hell! And get me off right now!" What occurs next is an unobserved technicality. His life, it so happens, is the source of pain and therefore what must be extinguished.

This is not to say the suicide puts no thought into how he will end his life. Most suicides do not result from some sudden, unpredictable or random act. In most cases, a suicide plan has developed over time and has been rehearsed in the person's mind several times. Fantasy-produced trial runs permit the prospective suicide to overcome potential obstacles to the plan. He strategizes but then fears that someone will sense something is up. What if they attempt to intervene? Or what if the plan fails to address how the survivors will react to the suicide? What if they discover the body? What will people say about my suicide? Maybe I should leave a note. Is there something I can do first, to alleviate their initial fears? This may go on for some while. The suicide wanna-be fights against his proposal, deserts the plan, and tries thinking other thoughts or busying himself with other acts. Regrettably, for some, nothing helps. The individual thus loses hope and returns once again to thoughts of suicide.[17] He is back where he started, and it is only a matter of time before the catalyst is set into motion and the discernible line between deliberating and acting suddenly vanishes.

The question we want to answer at this point concerns the suicide who is a believer. We can all understand the desire to escape one's pain. The decision to take one's life, however, strikes us as not only senseless but presumptuous. Even if we may believe that suicide does not result from giving up on God's grace, at the very least we would like to know whether this person was thinking about God and *his* assessment of things. But if a believer is on the brink of suicide, God may not even be on his radar. All he can think about is ridding himself of his terrible anguish. There is one thing that thrusts him to the other side. He lacks the necessary equipment to turn off the pain. Suicide is his only instrument of relief.

That moment Jean made the decision to take her life, was she thinking about how her *Lord* would react? I do not believe so. Jean was thinking about what in her mind had become intolerable. She would never overcome her depression and therefore never again be able to serve as mother to our children. She was thinking about the only way *she* could react under the circumstances to get her insufferable pain to stop. My comments about Jean, I know, will apply to many other Christians who have ended their lives. I am not going to say Jean was not thinking about God at all. The last thing on her mind, however, was rejecting Christ. I believe she was thinking about heaven. She believed Christ's promises concerning salvation. And she clung to these promises. Therefore, she was not fleeing *from* God's grace. It would be more accurate to say she was fleeing *to* God's grace. I believe she wanted to hear the Word again without the current diversion of unremitting hopelessness and suffering. She was "calling the question," her sense of being in question. I am sure this is not completely uncommon among believers who take their lives. The Christian concludes: "My only chance is if what I've learned about God's grace is true." For obvious reasons, you and I are incapable of drawing such a conclusion. As the suicide sees it, however, death is the only means of obtaining God's grace.

Notes

[1]James Hillman, *Suicide and the Soul* (Dallas: Spring Publications, Inc., 1979), p. 38.

[2]Ann Smolin, CSW; and John Guinan, PhD, *Healing After the Suicide of a Loved One* (New York: Simon & Schuster, Inc., 1993), p. 22.

[3]George Hoe Colt, *The Enigma of Suicide* (New York: Simon & Schuster, 1991), p. 205.

[4]David D. Burns, MD, *Feeling Good: The New Mood Therapy* (New York: Avon Books, Inc., 1980), p. 385.

[5]Eve Moscicki, reported by Rebecca Goldin, *The New York Times Perpetuates a Myth,* October 2004, http://www.stats.org (accessed January 30, 2006).

[6]David Sue, Derald Sue, and Stanley Sue, *Understanding Abnormal Behavior,* Fifth Edition (Boston, New York: Houghton Mifflin Company, 1997), p. 366.

[7]Robert E. Litman, MD; Edwin S. Shneidman, PhD; and Norman L. Farberow, PhD, *The Psychology of Suicide* (New York, London: Jason Aronson, Inc., 1983), p. 301.

[8]Details inspired by a conversation with Rev. Randy Taber, pastor of Olivet United Methodist Church in Robbinsdale, Minnesota, and Lt. Colonel in the National Guard.

[9]John Hewett, *After Suicide* (Philadelphia: The Westminster Press, 1952), p. 24.

[10]Edwin S. Shneidman, *The Suicidal Mind* (New York: Oxford University Press, Inc., 1996), p. 133.

[11]Edwin S. Shneidman, ed., *On the Nature of Suicide* (San Francisco: Jossey-Bass, Inc., 1969), p. 71.

[12]Burns, *Feeling Good,* p. 387.

[13]Shneidman, *The Suicidal Mind,* p. 7.

[14]Ibid., p. 13.

[15]Jeffrey S. Black, "Making Sense of the Suicide of a Christian," in *The Journal of Biblical Counseling,* Vol. 18, No. 3 (Philadelphia: Christian Counseling & Educational Foundation, Spring 2000).

[16]Shneidman, *The Suicidal Mind,* p. 134.

[17]Litman, *The Psychology of Suicide,* pp. 297,298.

Chapter 8

OVERCOMING THE DESIRE TO EXCUSE

We may consider it somewhat ironic. Today's culture in a sort of indirect way, perhaps unknowingly, has been more successful than the church in reducing suicide's stigma. It has happened, however, at a cost to the truth and the integrity of Scripture. There is no mention of the *sin* of suicide. However unreasonable it may be for people to refuse to acknowledge that Christians too commit suicide, we may not justify another extreme attitude. That is to make excuses for the believer rather than to acknowledge that Christians may be lured into sinful behavior. Having been informed on the subject, we must still address the act of suicide. As Christians, we may not explain away the suicide by reasoning: "It is so sad, but I am sure he did what he thought he had to in his situation." Understanding on our part does not constitute justification. We must define suicide in conformity with what it is, a grievous sin. Only then will we succeed in dealing with the enduring misconceptions about suicide and suicide's stigma.

In the previous chapter, we offered a comprehensive summary of how depressive illnesses, accumulative stresses, and traumatic events relate to suicide. Such a study is essential to comprehending the unbearable pain suffered by people who lose hope and choose to end their lives. In this chapter we answer: "Did he sin? If so, why did he *in this way* commit *this* sin? And finally, will God condemn him for this sin?"

Shall We Blame Genes?

 God created man and woman so that they might *cherish* life. And yet this person, being depressed, lost hope and *took* his life.

We confront another paradox. Whatever the cause or source of depression, God created man and woman and he saw that what he made was good. How does the Almighty's creation go bad despite his gracious plan for us? How can a person choose to inflict deadly harm on himself, when mankind was designed by God to value life and live out life according to his purpose? Even when life is burdensome and you lose your yearning for life, you do not take matters into your own hands and kill yourself! You may point out that you too have suffered under an oppressive form of depression. You even had thoughts about suicide. But you could not bring yourself to carry out what you were contemplating. So why were matters so different for this person who *did* take his life?

Psychologists and those associated with health and science professions generally agree that all or most suicides are amoral in nature. Suicides are most often associated with psychological and sociological factors and biochemistry. As Christians, however, we are obligated to acknowledge that suicides are also sinful. We agree that individuals are more subject or less subject to suicide depending on how they are affected psychologically, environmentally, and biologically. But we are also compelled to acknowledge the existence of "original sin," as the church has called it. To be distinguished from "actual sins" (the specific sins we commit with our thoughts, desires, words, and deeds), original sin is that total corruption of our whole human nature, which we have inherited from Adam through our parents.[1] David bemoaned the fact that he, and hence all of us, was sinful at birth, "sinful from the time my mother conceived me" (Psalm 51:5). A more explicit translation from the Hebrew reads that we were "*fashioned* in sin." That is to say, through the sinful nature of our parents, we were already sinful at the very time God was creating us and giving us life in the womb. This means each and every one of us from our very conception is corrupted thoroughly with sin. St. Paul also lamented: "I know that nothing good lives in me, that is, in my sinful nature" (Romans 7:18). Original sin affects not simply one's will, but one's entire being. Our human nature has not simply contracted some virus, which may potentially exhibit some undesirable symptoms in our lives. The extent of our sinfulness runs so deep that there is nothing left in body or soul that remains unaffected.

How did he get this way?

Each of us is unique because of how our sinful nature affects our person. Original sin, we must understand, affects not only our hearts and our wills. It affects each of us physically, emotionally, and psychologically in diverse and unique ways. We inherit from our parents what we might call "sin's fingerprint." Sin has marked each one of us a little bit differently. This does not mean some people inherit more sin than others or a worse form of sinfulness. Rather, how sin manifests itself will vary from person to person. In some way or another, our ability to function as God designed us is compromised.

You may have inherited, for example, a predisposition toward diabetes, Alzheimer's disease, heart disease, or cancer. Or as a personality trait, you may have inherited a predisposition for being extremely sensitive or emotional. It is also possible you are predisposed for being ill-tempered or unreasonable. As for myself, I believe I have inherited a predisposition for anxiety or nervousness. I personally get quite nervous when I am thrust into an unfamiliar setting. Although I am required as a pastor to be involved in public speaking, it is not my nature to speak with the confidence and assertiveness people may expect. Reflecting on our previously mentioned case studies, three out of the five had a predisposition for depression or mental illness. Jean, John, and Karl each had a blood relative who suffered from some kind of depressive disorder.

Keep in mind that the brain is like any other part of the body. It is affected by original sin. Depression, like all physical illnesses we suffer, results from being born a sinner in a fallen world. Every ailment of ours is symptomatic of the fact that our souls are sick and in need of healing. That healing is provided thankfully through the blood of Christ. It was for our transgressions that he was pierced, for our iniquities that he was crushed. It was and is by his wounds that we *are* healed (Isaiah 53:5). We are forgiven both for what we *do* (our actual sin) and for how we *are* (our original sin).

What I am driving at, plain and simple, is this: suicide is a sin. What is more, a person develops clinical depression because he is by nature sinful. However, the illness of clinical depression is not a sin. Depression merely causes a person to become vulnerable in various ways, not in a spiritual sense, in the sense that his faith becomes less protected against grave temptation. He becomes vulnerable to a sense of hopelessness. He is not able to evaluate in a normal manner the circumstances affecting his life. Pessimism dominates his thoughts so that he is capable of constructing only a negative outlook on tomorrow and, very possibly, on the rest of his life.

Can God's Word cure depression and other mental health problems?

I expect pastors of Christ's church today will remain mindful of an obvious responsibility. You must help your people distinguish between what God is capable of doing and what you may believe he will do—what he promises and what he does not promise. For example, Christ promises forgiveness and eternal life to those who believe in him. In accordance with his will, he promises to provide for me richly and on a daily basis "all that I need to support this body and life."[2] What he does not promise is to heal me because I have faith in his Word and his ability to make me better. Despite the claims of certain people today, including many faith-healing cults, there are thousands of people who have a strong faith in their Savior, yet God in his wisdom has willed that they not be healed in this life.

Normally, a person cannot expect that God's Word will cure his depression. One exception may be if his depression is not chemically induced but relates to a guilty conscience. If you recall a recent event where you, having been brought to a knowledge of our sin, were trying to cope with a guilt-oriented depression, you may also recall being comforted by the gospel. A family member, a fellow parishioner, or a pastor told you that God has forgiven you. You believed their words and your depression was replaced with needed comfort to your soul.

If your sense of guilt takes on the form of depression, you know you are in good company. Martin Luther suffered on occasion from a very deep form of depression for days and even weeks. It was induced by his acute awareness of his sin. His religious upbringing had taught him that salvation was possible only for those whose numerous sins were removed through penance, praying to the saints, and other sacred observances, such as making pilgrimages to various shrines. Even after Luther discovered that sinners are justified by faith apart from the works of the law (Romans 3:28), he went through great pains attempting to remember his many sins so that he might confess them and be absolved. His depression, it is evident, prompted him to obtain consolation from the gospel. Luther would find himself sad and discouraged and would get rid of his depression by crying out to himself, *"Vivit!"* the Latin for "He lives!" Many times he grabbed a piece of chalk and wrote this *Vivit* not only on his study table but all over the walls and doors of his study. When someone asked him why he did this, he answered, "Jesus lives, and if he were not among the living, I would not wish to live one hour; but because he lives, we shall live through him, as he himself says, 'Because I live, you shall live also.'"[3]

Like the reformer, you too may subdue your depression by turning to Scripture to hear of Christ's forgiveness. Sometimes, however, it would be inappropriate to infer that a healthy reading of God's Word will alleviate a person's depression. Sometimes guilt is induced by a misinformed conscience. It may be that the person's medication is not working properly. His thinking has been altered, and though he imagines being a certain way or doing something that has offended others, there is no basis for it.

I remember when Jean's depression first became quite severe. She had been prescribed various medications but nothing had proved beneficial. There was this dark secret she could not bring herself to talk about. No doubt her distorted thinking was feeding her with misinformation. I often wish I had talked more about the faith we shared and recited to her comforting passages from the Bible. When I did read to her, she seemed to do a little better. But it did not last. The dirty little secret kept seeping back into her thoughts.

Karl had also been plagued by intense guilt. All his life he had adopted very high standards when it came to being the family's breadwinner. His wife and family depended on him, and he was not about to let his children down now because of some health issues. But ultimately he would, according to his conscience that is. Karl had an unrealistic judgment of his abilities. His arthritis and brain tumor would frustrate his efforts to keep up with his apparent duties. But he was never able to admit this to himself.

If you are uninformed regarding depression, you may easily misdiagnose the problem of another believer and offer questionable aid. If you are psychologically healthy yourself, you may lack understanding regarding the believer who is suffering from a sense of guilt. You may also be tempted to give the person some questionable advice. "If I just remind him about the love of his Savior, who saves and never leaves our side, surely his guilty feelings will subside." But what if you are mistaken and nothing changes?

Just because the gospel has the power to *cover up* sin, does not mean it is necessarily going to remove the *effects* of sin. I would love to help you get rid of your migraine by citing to you John 3:16. But it does not work that way. The good news about our Savior will not eliminate one's predisposition for depression any more than it will provide an immunity against heart disease. It will not take away my fear of speaking in an unfamiliar setting any more than it will temper your aversion to anchovies. Extreme sadness, a low sense of self-worth, and a feeling of hopelessness are not in every case caused by sinful behavior. Books and articles, moreover, which promise relief for those experiencing mild or moderate forms of depression and say nothing to those suffering from clinical depression about the need for medication or therapy are performing a tremendous disservice. Telling a person "Your depression can be overcome if you get into the Word and witness how God works faith and healing" is more than misguided advice. Such counsel is deceptive and may potentially place the depressed individual at a greater risk. How is he supposed to feel, after all, when after being told that the Word will cure him, he notes no change? More than likely he will blame it on his faith; he did not believe in the power of the Word. That obviously will not do a great deal to ease his depression.

Overcoming clinical depression has little or nothing to do with hearing God's Word. What may prove effective in restoring a healthy functioning of the brain are antidepressant medications and psychotherapy —whether provided jointly or independently. I know someone who undergoes psychotherapy every two to three weeks with a doctor of psychology and visits a psychiatrist every three months for evaluation and medication therapy as a way of monitoring his thoughts. By the same token, sometimes people must rely on trial-and-error efforts. Antidepressants may or may not help a particular individual. Therapy for many depressed people is begun with the understanding that depression stems from negative and self-destructive patterns of thinking. Often this harmful thinking has taken many years to develop. When patients are made aware of these patterns, they may be instructed in new ways of thinking and work at overcoming their distorted thinking.

Suicide and Accountability

 Sinners are accountable for every sin they commit. Yet this person was apparently not responsible for his actions.

A red flag is raised as we become conscious of another paradox with regard to the suicide. We know most certainly that God must condemn all sin. Are you to say, however, that people born with various predispositions may *not* be responsible for their actions? The facts are in, after all. It has been determined that the person could not help despairing and one thing led to another.

Sometimes we play games with God. We question whether every sin is in fact a sin. Whether a given act is right or wrong, we want to believe is open to interpretation. That is how many people will treat the sin of suicide. He was sick, and beyond that we cannot make any judgment. I am reminded of a meeting I had with an attorney after Jean's death. He was confident he could help me collect what I deserved under Jean's life insurance policy. The company was refusing to pay the entire amount since she died by suicide. He proposed that we could collect the full benefits of the policy if we maintained that Jean's suicide was by accident. I promptly refused his offer. I was not going to pretend that my wife had other intentions than taking her life. The truth would have to have the final say in this matter. To this day, I have no idea whether the attorney's efforts would have proved successful. What I do know is that the surviving family of a suicide might present a similar argument to our judge in heaven. If the evidence reveals that he was not in his right mind, perhaps the Lord will agree that it was simply an unfortunate incident, an accident, if you will. Therefore, he should not be held accountable.

All explanations considered, was he accountable?

Yes, he sinned and therefore he was accountable. Every Christian must concur. Regardless of who we are, we may never claim that we have no choice but to do what is wrong. Every person sins with the consent of his will. "Each one is tempted when, by his own evil desire, he is dragged away and enticed" (James 1:14). Despite our discussion concerning original sin and its potential effect on the human psyche, we are always accountable as sinners before God. Yes, it may be that we are not always accountable from a *human* standpoint. A convicted killer enters a plea that he is innocent by reason of insanity. The court concurs that he did not know what he was doing. Therefore, he is not accountable for his grievous crime. Nevertheless, even if something is not a crime according to human law, it *may* be a sin. Suicide has been defined as an act of the will whereby a person wills his own death and succeeds in getting his own way.[4] Understanding suicide in this way, it must be called a sin. Irrespective of whether the suicide was of the right mind, he exerted his will over God's will. He broke God's command: "You shall not murder" and is therefore accountable for his sin.

Despite one's inability to perceive what is real or not real, we may never assert: "My disease made me do it!" There is never a vagueness concerning God's will. Under God's law, the entire world, every sinner, is accountable to God. St. Paul affirms this by saying, "Now we know that whatever the law says, it says to those who are under the law, so that every mouth may be silenced and the whole world held accountable to God" (Romans 3:19). You and I are accountable under God's law, and we are accountable for *every* sin we commit. Thank Christ that we are saved, not by exercising our sick will but by grace through faith.

105

There is something else that may make it difficult to be objective about a particular suicide and acknowledge that the person sinned. The world tends to judge the gravity of a crime based on how many will be affected by it, rather than simply to judge the crime for the act that it is. This suggests that we may sometimes respond with anger and repugnance and other times sorrow and sympathy, depending on the nature of the offense. But Scripture teaches that a sin is a sin is a sin. Likewise, a suicide is a suicide is a suicide. It is no less a suicide if the survivors have reason to sympathize with the suicide's motives. Nor is it less a sin if its impact on family and friends is minimized, since, despite its dreadful nature, they are able to adjust and move on with their lives.

Every suicide is accountable for the sin of suicide. But *why* is he accountable? Is it because of his ability to make the right choice? No. A suicide is accountable because God's law is written in his heart. True, the decision is misguided. A Christian kills himself believing things are hopeless, to the point of no return. Nevertheless, every suicide is accountable for his sin.

Is suicide an unforgivable sin?

It is a question you would prefer to answer neither before nor after the fact. If a suicide is accountable for his suicide, what will God make of his sin? How will God react to his killing himself? Was the early church correct in its assessment that the suicide was going to hell? If you are troubled whether God will condemn the sin of suicide, let me submit that your real question is, Are there different kinds of sins and do some sins carry more serious consequences? The answer is, yes. But before I get specific, remember that according to Scripture all sin is rebellion against God and deserves eternal damnation, even the sins of believers. Scripture teaches that "all have sinned and fall short of the glory of God" (Romans 3:23). Even Christians fall short of God's glory on a daily basis and are, in fact, sinning continually.

But if this is indeed the case, how can you maintain that Christians *alone* may hope for eternal life with Christ? It is on this point that you must distinguish between various sins. The church traditionally has spoken of mortal and venial sins. Venial sins are those, which although committed daily by believers and those deserving of eternal death, are also forgiven each day to the believer. Sins committed every day by believers have also been referred to as sins of weakness, which emerge and spring forth out of ignorance or rashness.[5] The sin is involuntary—not in the sense that a Christian did not desire or intend to do what he did—but because he did not willfully ignore the accusations of his conscience. Sins of weakness consist of all evil thoughts, desires, feelings, words, and deeds that emerge in the lives of Christians and are caused by their sinful nature, which works in opposition to their will.[6] Such sins, in the end, do not destroy faith because they do not drive the Holy Spirit from the heart.[7]

Mortal sins, on the other hand, are those sins that result in eternal death. Such sins include the sins of unbelievers and those of believers who force the Holy Spirit out of the heart. Luther has written: "But if anyone sins knowingly, by design, and willingly because of some presumption, and despises the threats and wrath of God, he commits a mortal sin."[8] Are there particular sins that come to mind here? Not necessarily. Any sin may become mortal if a person presumes, despite the warnings of the conscience, that he is justified in demonstrating a disregard for God's will.

A similar distinction may be made between "ruling sins" (Hebrews 10:26,27) committed by unbelievers and "ruled sins" that are present in the lives of believers. Ruling sins are those where Satan is the ruling power in them.[9] They exist in those who are dead in sin (Ephesians 2:1) and by nature resist the Holy Spirit (Acts 7:51). Ruled sins are carried out by Christians, whose spirit continues to battle against the sinful nature. As a believer, naturally, you are aware of this indwelling and ongoing battle and do not desire to justify what goes against your will and conscience. St. Paul exhorts you to this end, saying, "Therefore do not let sin reign in your mortal body so that you obey its evil desires. . . . For sin shall not be your master, because you are not under law, but under grace" (Romans 6:12,14). Regrettably, Christians do on occasion give in to or are overcome by a ruling sin. It happens when a believer permits himself to become a slave to sin and temptation; when he knowingly permits himself to be dragged away and enticed (James 1:14).

So what shall we say concerning the sin of suicide committed by a believer? Understand that it is not the enormity of a sin that causes people to fall from grace and lose their faith, but the attitude that the heart has toward the sin.[10] C. F. W. Walther, a nineteenth-century theologian and seminary president, once had this to say about sins that have the power to squelch faith.

> When I am suddenly overtaken by sin, God forgives me. . . . Such acts do not extinguish my faith. Or it may be that I am rushed into sin by my temperament. I do not want to sin, but I

have been irritated to such an extent that, before I know it, I have sinned. That is not a mortal sin, which would take me out of the state of grace. But when a person persists in his sin against his conscience, though he knows it to be a sin, and continues sinning purposely for a long time, he no longer has faith and cannot truly pray to God; the Holy Spirit leaves his heart, for another spirit, the evil spirit, rules in it, whom the sinner has admitted into his heart. To him the Holy Spirit yields his place and departs.[11]

It is not reasonable to conclude that the believer who took his life following a severe bout of depression or absolute hopelessness did so because he drove the Holy Spirit from his heart. A more accurate assessment will go something like this: He was convinced he would never see life again from a positive standpoint. For a while he battled the urge to resign his life. The struggle was intense and as time progressed seemed increasingly futile. Eventually he determined that it was unbearable and decided to concede to the luring call within. He finally committed suicide, not because his fight to resist evil came to a slow or abrupt halt, not because the struggle was replaced with a ruling sin. Rather, he was no longer able to wait for the pain to go away.

You may call to mind a couple of the suicides I referenced earlier, both whom were Christian. Brian caused his own death by overdosing on a barbiturate. He was found you will remember in complete uniform. John was one of at least two hundred people who committed suicide by jumping from one of the twin towers on 9/11. He was later identified when his body was recovered and a couple forms of identification were retrieved. In either case, it did not matter how foolproof the plan was, how quickly the death occurred, or how pretty this person would appear afterward. In neither case were they overcome by a "ruling sin." It was out of weakness and desperation that the two resolved that they were not capable of delaying their deaths any longer.

I am not justifying what these gentlemen did. *Before* we commit sin, we may not condone a sinful deed supposing Jesus will forgive. "Shall we go on sinning so that grace may increase?" the apostle asks. "By no means! We died to sin; how can we live in it any longer?" (Romans 6:1,2). However, *after* we sin by weakness of our flesh, we may believe we are forgiven. Having been humbled by God's law and a knowledge of our sin, we may receive the comfort Christ gives in his gospel. Inasmuch as Christ has indeed *paid* for every sin, we may believe that we are *forgiven* of every sin. And so may we believe regarding our fellow Christian who commits suicide. "[Christ] is the atoning sacrifice for our sins, and not only for ours but also for the sins of the *whole world*" (1 John 2:2).

Did he really have time to repent?

People ask this question out of ignorance. Even if it has been explained to them what sins may be designated unforgivable and it has been determined that suicide is not such a sin, there is that paradox which so far has gone unresolved. A Christian will make an effort to confess every sin he can remember. Yet this Christian, having committed suicide, deprived himself of the chance to do so.

As you surely have noted, some attempt to resolve the paradox of a Christian's suicide by stating that because of the time factor and the suicide's inability to repent, he must be in hell. If time were a matter of relevance, however, each of us would be in grave trouble. Every one of us is a sinner. That means we sin perpetually. We also all die as sinners, since the wages of sin is death (Romans 6:23). Meanwhile, there is no remedy for our sinful condition here on earth. Our only hope is the resurrection of all believers, which we are promised will take place on the Last Day. Then we will be glorified, becoming perfect in every sense of the word.

Even so, people have serious issues when professing Christians die shortly after committing a tragic sin. "We'd better not be too quick to acknowledge such people as believers. We may undermine the importance of repentance and give the impression that it is not necessary in every case." But this is not true unless you assert that repentance is something more than what Scripture describes. *Repentance,* as the term is used in Scripture, means "changing one's mind." A sinner changes his mind about sin and about trusting in his own deeds to save him. He is sorry for his sins and believes Jesus Christ to be his Savior. But you need to determine how this is possible. How does one confess his sin and trust in his Savior rather than himself? How does one *change one's mind?* The answer is, God works repentance as he works faith. He works it in the believer through his Word. Paul writes Timothy concerning a workman approved by God, telling him that those who oppose him, "he must gently instruct, in the hope that God will grant them repentance" (2 Timothy 2:25). Yes, the Christian is the one who does the repenting just as he is the one who does the believing. However, both are gifts from God, which he works in us through his messages of sin and grace.

When you think of repentance as your work rather than God's work, your entire concept of repentance is altered. Repentance becomes your way of making up for a recent sin. You repent in order to regain God's approval. Sadly, such repentance is very unreliable, since as a sinner you keep slipping back into your old ways. At best you may think of repentance as an on-and-off switch. Your switch is on so long as you are reflecting on the grace of God who forgives you through Jesus Christ. It is on as long as you are living an obedient life. And your switch is off once you slip into sin, albeit out of weakness. As for the suicide who was a Christian, presumably the switch was flicked off just before he carried out the act.

Such an assumption, however, is both unfortunate and wrong. You may not presume that a suicide, since he has no time to confess his sin after he kills himself, therefore has no chance of being saved. The question is whether or not he was a Christian. Can a believer commit a shameful sin and remain a believer? Let me answer that question by making two points. First, it is a given that faith and the refusal to repent cannot coincide. The believer who willingly and persistently continues in sin does more than place his faith in jeopardy. He sentences his faith to death. Such was the case with King David, whose refusal to repent led him from lust to adultery and finally to murder. As the days passed, David, having kept silent, complained that his bones had wasted away through his groaning all day long (Psalm 32:3). Refusing to repent, his faith could no longer console him. The truth is, he had *fallen* from faith. When David, however, was later confronted with his sin, by the grace of God he repented. The second point is relevant with respect to the believer who commits suicide. The final question is not whether he had *time* to repent but whether he *refused* to repent, and we cannot make that assertion. True, time did not permit him to repent after he sinned. But bear in mind that repentance is God's work. Therefore, time ran out not on the Christian but on God, if we may speak that way.

The tragedy of suicide reminds us of how thankful we can be that we are not all on our own, spiritually speaking. Yes, Christians are individuals who freely, without compulsion, repent of their sins each day. However, we are saved not by our acts of repentance, which we hope to generate around the clock. We are saved because "the blood of Jesus, his Son, purifies us from *all* sin" (1 John 1:7).

There is a more appropriate remark to be made when a Christian dies by suicide. Instead of asserting, "He had no chance in the final moments to repent!" we may state, "We had no chance in the final moments to see his faith." It is common at a Christian funeral if the deceased died suddenly to hear someone lament, "I had no chance to say good-bye." Proving just as disheartening for Christian survivors, including survivors of a suicide, is having no chance to hear a confession of faith. We would have preferred hearing their assurance, "Don't you worry. I'll be with my Savior soon!" Such words of comfort, however, are left for the family to share with one another. Your words may sound something like this: "Yes, she sinned and has paid the price with her life. But Christ paid for her sin. He kept her in the faith. And now she is in heaven!"

Notes

[1]*Luther's Small Catechism With Explanation,* p. 96.

[2]Ibid., First Article, p. 13.

[3]Oswald Riess, *Everlasting Arms: Sermons for Festivals and Special Occasions* (New York, Chicago: Ernst Kaufmann, Inc., 1949), p. 87.

[4]Shneidman, *On the Nature of Suicide,* p. 123.

[5]Francis Pieper, *Christian Dogmatics,* Vol. 1 (St. Louis: Concordia Publishing House, 1950), pp. 565,566.

[6]Ibid.

[7]Ibid., p. 567.

[8]*Luther's Works,* Vol. 8, p. 50.

[9]Pieper, *Christian Dogmatics,* Vol. 1, p. 568.

[10]C. F. W. Walther, *The Proper Distinction Between Law and Gospel* (hereafter cited as *Law and Gospel*), edited and translated by W. H. T. Dau (St. Louis: Concordia Publishing House, 1928), p. 220.

[11]Ibid.

Chapter 9

YOU MEAN HE'S IN HEAVEN?

 A Christian, by definition, is living in a state of grace. Yet this Christian was overcome by the power of sin.

The previous two chapters have explained that the paradox relating to a Christian's suicide cannot be resolved outside a proper understanding of sin, its nature and consequences. We cannot talk about suicide at any length without discussing its association with depression. Suicide is primarily psychological. Preceding chapters also state that suicide is not linked to some kind of spiritual deficiency. There might very well be no connection between a given suicide and that person's faith or lack of faith.

Before we complete our discussion of this matter, however, we need to say a little more about the paradox of a Christian's suicide. There is more to this subject than a comprehensive study of the nature and role of faith and a thorough explanation of original sin. There is more to talk about than establishing why people lose hope and develop a desire to end their lives. We need to explore the nature of God's relationship with believers who give in to the sin of suicide. If someone asks us why we believe their loved one is in heaven, and they are hoping for a sound biblical answer, what shall we tell them? Knowing what we do about God's grace, we can reassure them that this family member, who was a Christian, is with his Savior.

Grace, correctly understood, is God's disposition of favor toward sinners. It relates *both* to God's love for us sinners and his intent to save us. God saves you not because you deserve to be saved. He saves you despite your sinful nature and the sins you commit. He saves you because it is his gracious will to save and grant his salvation as a gift. The apostle writes in Ephesians, "It is by grace you have been saved, through faith—and this not from yourselves, it is the gift of God—not by works, so that no one can boast" (2:8,9). In addition, the gift of grace cannot be understood apart from the person and work of Jesus Christ. Grace is the mercy of God by which believers are accepted for the sake of Christ's sacrifice. Despite the fact that you are an absolute sinner, our heavenly Father loves you and saves you because his Son paid the ransom for your sins. Although "all have sinned and fall short of the glory of God" (Romans 3:23), all "are justified freely by his grace through the redemption that came by Christ Jesus" (verse 24).

Jesus is also the reason you can be confident you will *remain* saved by God's grace. To be saved by grace is to live your life in a *state of grace*. The Lord is committed to seeing that nothing compromises your faith in Christ. Having *called* you to faith through Christ's gospel, he will *sustain* you in the faith through his gospel. The apostle Peter speaks of an inheritance that is "kept in heaven for you, who through faith are shielded by God's power until the coming of the salvation that is ready to be revealed in the last time" (1 Peter 1:4,5).

We are confronted with a final paradox when it becomes evident that this person who took his life was living in a state of grace. The Lord was earnestly sustaining him in his faith. And yet he was overcome by a sin that suggests he had lost his faith. People have tried to resolve the paradox by drawing one of two conclusions. One possibility is that the suicide was no longer living under God's grace. In the time of need, he rejected the Lord's grace, choosing his own method of dealing with his difficulties. The other possibility is that God's grace was not sufficient in his case to sustain him in faith and thus save him. He gave up on God and took his life, since God's grace was not up to the task of keeping him on the straight and narrow.

Ignorance concerning the suicide of Christians is largely due to the fact that people have never been instructed properly regarding a workable definition of God's saving grace. Some imagine that saving grace is God's method of empowering a believer to do the right thing or make the right choice. When Scripture declares that God saves by grace, what comes to mind for them is not God's unmerited love for sinners but that which God infuses into a believer's heart to help him live a Christian life. It is believed that God's grace arouses the Christian to do good works and aids him in his efforts to avoid sinful behavior. The Lord's saving grace, as it were, relates not to the forgiveness of sins but to the betterment of one's spiritual life.

The saving grace of God, properly understood, does not concern Christian conduct. It relates to who Christ is and what he has achieved for us sinners. It has to do with the conduct of our Savior, who having lived a perfect life for us also gave up his life for us. Having said that, there is a definite correlation between God's disposition toward a given sinner and whether the same sinner will remain in the faith when his faith is tested. God's grace and what it means to live in a "state of grace" are properly understood when you have a correct understanding of the "means of grace." The means of grace are the means by which God keeps you believing and benefiting from his grace. They are the gospel and the sacraments. You may think of them as God's instruments through which the Lord confers the forgiveness of sins and strengthens one's faith. Accordingly, those who remain in the faith in the direst circumstances are not pumped up disciples who have learned the secret of resisting temptation. They are simple Christians who have heard Christ's message of forgiveness. They are believers who have participated in the body and blood of their Savior in Holy Communion. They are sinners who are baptized.

God is not one who watches from the sidelines, hoping for the best. He is in charge of our souls. To remain in the state of grace has this meaning: inasmuch as you sin perpetually, Christ has determined that you receive his forgiveness perpetually. As the corruption of your human nature is absolute, so must his grace be absolute. So intent is Christ on saving you that he uses his gospel and sacraments to keep you from falling. St. Paul affirms: "May your whole spirit, soul and body be kept blameless at the coming of our Lord Jesus Christ. The one who calls you is faithful and he will do it" (1 Thessalonians 5:23,24). It does not matter how critical your circumstances, your Savior will not desert you so that you must deal with your sinful condition yourself.

Many pastors, unfortunately, do not direct suffering and hopeless people to the gospel and sacraments. Although pastors may assert that God saves a sinner by grace, they do not see God's *gifts* of grace as having the power to furnish forgiveness and faith. God's grace rather is regarded as that by which a Christian is enabled to stand on his own and follow his conscience rather than do something self-destructive. And should a Christian take his life? Once again, there are two possibilities. Either the Christian was not up to the challenge or God's grace was not up to the challenge. In any event, his sin overtook him, faith and all.

I Believe! Help Me in My Unbelief!

Can a person believe at the very time that he's struggling with unbelief?

My wife related to me more than once that she was in torment because of a spiritual struggle. She asked me, "Will I go to heaven if I don't wait for God? Can I be saved if I take my life?" As much as she feared losing her faith in Christ, I do not believe her fears had any

115

basis. However, inside of her she was engaged in a conflict of sorts. And she was convinced it had a direct relation to her faith.

The question of whether a bona fide Christian can commit suicide is really a question of whether he can believe in his Savior and at the same time wrestle with unbelief. The answer is, yes. Understand that there is more to living in a state of grace than obtaining perpetual forgiveness. God also gives you the means to hold on to his forgiveness. This is an enormous comfort, given that it is your nature as a sinner, even after you have been converted, not to believe. When the Holy Spirit gives you faith through the gospel, this act of regeneration does not change who you are by nature. You are still very much a sinner who has every inclination not to believe but to do evil (Genesis 8:21). St. Paul affirms this, saying that the sinful nature "desires what is contrary to the Spirit, and the Spirit what is contrary to the sinful nature. They are in conflict with each other, so that you do not do what you want" (Galatians 5:17). That is why you depend upon God's grace and why Christ has supplied his church with the means of grace. Despite the fact that you are a believer and the Spirit works in you the will to do only what is pleasing to God, you are still prone to resist the Spirit's will.

Every Christian is familiar with the battle between the sinful nature, or "the flesh," and the Spirit. Some, however, I am convinced are more conscious of the battle than others. You may consider a man who once sought help from the Lord Jesus, as his son was possessed by a demon. When Jesus challenged the man for his apparent lack of faith, he answered the Lord, "I do believe; help me overcome my unbelief!" (Mark 9:24). The father had spoken truthfully. He believed in Christ and his ability to rescue his son from Satan's hold. However, he was still staring in the face the realities of his son's possession. In order for the father to enjoy victory in his struggle against unbelief, it was essential that he hear from the Lord his promise of deliverance. Like this father and like those suffering from depression, you too are involved in a constant struggle. On the one hand, you are convinced you are forgiven. On the other hand, you still come face-to-face with the realities of your sin. You *do* believe. Your faith in Jesus Christ is absolutely genuine inasmuch as it is created and sustained by God's Word and sacraments. However, your faith is always mixed with unbelief.

Even so, you cannot presume that if disturbed individuals are more conscious of their struggle or it is more intense, they inevitably will have a greater chance of losing their faith. You might consider it a poor reflection on your faith should you *not* experience an ongoing struggle. Paul once preached, "We *must* go through many hardships to enter the kingdom of God" (Acts 14:22). The difficulties you experience as a Christian do not indicate that you are *losing* the battle, merely that you are *engaged* in a battle. And all indications propose this battle will never end. The apostle laments, "When I want to do good, evil is right there with me. For in my inner being I delight in God's law; but I see another law at work in the members of my body, waging war against the law of my mind and making me a prisoner of the law of sin at work within my members" (Romans 7:21-23). You constantly must encounter struggles in your battle against the flesh. If you do not, it can only mean you are either giving in or you are giving up.

But what shall we deduce when a depressed Christian loses the will to fight and he begins to think of ways to end the battle between the Spirit and the flesh? It is not that the believer has abandoned the faith, having walked off the battlefield and gone AWOL as a Christian. More than likely he has already resisted the urge to end his life a number of times. But he hasn't determined how to put a stop to the temptation once and for all. However determined the despairing person may be to fight the temptation to carry out his suicide, the yearning to die does not just go away. Sometimes the temptation may lurk for weeks and months in the thoughts he keeps top secret. Even when he identifies the temptation, perhaps sensing it before him at all times, he does not necessarily see that day coming when the enemy finally has his way with him.

It is true in the case of every Christian. The conflict between your sinful nature and your inner being will continue. In your perpetual struggle against unbelief, you will on occasion become weak and give into a sin you had every good intension of avoiding. At such times, you do not make excuses. You do not boast that you'll do better the next round. Confessing your sin, you simply remember what it means to live in a state of grace. You also acknowledge Christ's first desire in your life. It is not to make you bold in your struggle against sin and temptation, as important as this may be. Neither is it to make you sure your faith is up to snuff. His highest desire is to give you his forgiveness and make you sure of *it*. True, the conflict between your flesh and the Spirit will continue the rest of your life, since there is nothing you can do to end the conflict. Although you want to do good, evil is always right there with you (Romans 7:21), seeking to drive you to despair. By God's grace, however, you may acknowledge your wretchedness as a sinner and ask, "Who will rescue me from this body of death? Thanks be to God—through Jesus Christ our Lord!" (Romans 7:24,25).

Where Sin Increased, Grace Increased All the More

How can a person remain a Christian if, due to his illness, he cannot hear God's Word?

It can be extremely discouraging to witness. The mother of the house refuses to get out of bed on Sunday morning as the rest of the family is getting ready for church. She used to be the one getting the others going each Sunday. Now she's telling them, "Leave me alone! You go without me today!" The husband tries to remind her of the blessings she will receive when she attends the weekly service. "Everybody needs to hear God's Word," he tells her. "We need to hear how we've sinned. And we need to hear how Christ has obtained forgiveness for us. 'Faith comes by hearing'" (Romans 10:17). But there she lies in the same position in which he found her sleeping. No one is going to change her mind. Struggling under the effects of her illness, she has no ambition to take on the day. The husband may guarantee her the greatest blessings on earth if she will simply spend a few moments getting herself ready and into the car. She'll see! But his words have no impact. She has neither the motivation nor the energy to get herself out of bed, reach for the doorknob, and peek behind door number 1. After a while, the family can be heard getting into the car. They choose to leave her behind, thinking that perhaps their Christian example will make a difference when next Sunday arrives. Unfortunately, little if anything changes.

Faith without hearing

I may point out that even if a person is successful in getting a depressed loved one to church, as I was, the depressed person may hear little or nothing of the service. He may instead reflect on the latest set of conclusions he has drawn under his illness. The greatest problem may not be his lack of get-up-and-go on a given Sunday morning, seeking out God's Word. He just is not hearing God's Word. A depressed individual develops a sort of tunnel vision with respect to his thought processes. He is no longer able to reflect on the blessings God bestows on him each day. In his view, his life can only head in one direction, the same downward track. His future no longer holds the same range of possibilities. Though nothing substantial in his life has really changed in recent weeks or months, he is not capable of

118

anticipating improvement in the situation. All he can think about is what he perceives is wrong with himself and his life. "I'm a lousy father *because* . . . My children don't want to be around me *because* . . . My parents don't trust me *because* . . . I'll never hold another job *because* . . ." Whatever the case may be, the same thoughts are being played over and over again with the result that God's message concerning a Savior is not reaching him. The gospel simply will not penetrate his pestering thoughts.

A most troubling development triggers a most troubling question. What if your loved one's struggles get so bad that he can no longer hear God's Word or he has no *modus operandi* by which he may go to God's Word for help? Many would assert about Christians who resort to suicide that had they been more faithful in seeking God's help through his Word and sacraments, they would still be with us today. They would not have lost hope. They would have chosen a less drastic method of dealing with their despair. What some would have us believe, apparently, is that a person cannot remain in a severely depressed state for an indefinite period of time without suffering spiritual consequences.

We may be reminded of the "grace period" we are granted as we shop for a car. There is no interest for a whole year! We do not have to make a payment for six months! The auto dealer extends this gesture of kindness hoping to generate business among those who are strapped for cash and might shop somewhere else otherwise. But six months pass and that once compassionate business takes on a different face. It does not matter that you have suddenly met with difficult times—you have lost your job and your mortgage payments have increased dramatically. No amount of complaining or excuse making will make any difference. If you do not resolve your troubles immediately, it's too bad. As luck would have it, your struggles have simply lasted too long. Time's up!

It would seem, as far as some are concerned, that God too is bound to some sort of grace period. A Christian can be overwhelmed by his struggles for only so long. A person can go only so long without hearing and comprehending God's Word. God's grace then expires, and he's on his own. This, sadly, leaves us with a question: What shall we make of this Christian who fails to deal suitably with his illness? He sleeps more than he is awake. He prefers keeping to himself. He will do nearly anything to avoid assembling with others.

Shall we conclude that because this Christian is suffering from the illness of depression, because no counseling or medication known to him will help him overcome his disease, and because he hasn't the wherewithal to get himself to church, his faith is in jeopardy? Or worse, shall we brand him an unbeliever insofar as he lacks the motivation or zeal to attend services, open a Bible, or seek spiritual support from his pastor? Hardly. Christ places us in a state of grace not because we have *time* for his grace. He positions us in his grace because we are weak and frail sinners and we *need* his grace. That is exactly why St. Paul assures us in his epistle to the Romans that "where sin increased, grace increased all the more" (Romans 5:20). Where sin puts faith in harm's way, grace puts Christ's forgiveness in our hearts.

A more appropriate analogy can be cited. An extremely depressed Christian in some cases may be compared to someone in a comatose state. Only the Christian's condition is better understood as a *walking* coma. As busy as he is, making it here and there and interacting with those around him, something is off. What is being said to him about the family, work at the office, or the weather barely reaches his consciousness. His preoccupation has monopolized his thought processes, and he is simply not able to think about anything else. Even if his family takes him to church, he gets no more out of it than a nursing home resident who has been in a coma for several years. Even so, a person in a coma may have faith. The severely depressed person is not necessarily rejecting God's Word. The problem is, any relevant message from God's Word is not reaching him.

Faith without feeling

The question about faith may have a different context. The problem may not have to do with getting a person to church to hear the Word. Or if he is getting to the service, the problem may not be that he is failing to hear the Word because of his internal distractions. Sometimes a depressed believer concludes that the message just isn't meant for him. He's not feeling encouraged by it. Despite the good news he is being told, he is not *feeling* anything as a result. A Christian with a severe case of depression may sometimes have enormous difficulty applying the gospel to his personal situation. He yearns to obtain the comfort only the gospel can provide. He does not despise the gospel. He simply is not feeling its relevance. He does not believe that it relates to him as much as it does someone else.

Most who experience major depression become pessimistic about life with respect to its earthly benefits. They do not believe that they can retrieve life's basic joys or pleasures. Life as such is dismal and meaningless. Some who are severely depressed may also become pessimistic in a spiritual respect. They may imagine that God's disposition toward them is not what it once was. "Why should I believe I'm God's child? He has no desire to bless me! He hates me!" When the effects of depression are quite severe, they may even conclude: "God has rejected me! He can't possibly forgive me for what I've done!"

Can a Christian remain a believer when he is evidently unwilling to apply the gospel to himself? Be assured in such cases that impaired thinking is speaking, not faith. The person is reacting not to the facts but to his *assessment* of the facts and how that is making him feel.

I remember a call I made several years ago when I was a pastor near Mayville, Wisconsin. I visited a woman in the hospital who had become quite agitated and irrational as evidenced by her comments to me. Referring to the doctors who had been treating her, she exclaimed, "They're trying to take my religion away!" I assured her that no one could touch her faith and then I believe I read to her, from the gospel of John, the words of Jesus: "My sheep listen to my voice; I know them. . . . I give them eternal life, and they shall never perish; no one can snatch them out of my hand" (John 10:27,28). The woman was obviously not to be deprived of her religion. She was not losing her faith. Her perception of reality was causing her to despair. And in time her condition did improve. However, I know better than to believe that I had something to do with it. It was not my words that eased her despair. It was the change in her medication prescribed by the doctors.

People who are ill mentally or emotionally may have enormous difficulty making sense out of God's promises. They see the Word of Christ as having no relevance for their circumstances. This is not to say that they have stopped thinking about Christ and his teachings. However, an individual may sometimes give his depression a spiritual application, i.e., "I'm despairing because something's wrong with my faith," or "I'm feeling hopeless, and life has become burdensome because God is punishing me." Such irrational despair does not certify that God's Word can no longer service his faith. We must not conclude that the person who believes God has rejected him has in fact rejected God. He may simply lack the mental capacity to relate the gospel to his personal situation.

God is able to sustain faith when a Christian loses his ability for rational thought and normal feelings. Moreover, the method by which the Lord preserves faith is always the same. He keeps Christians believing through the preaching and teaching of his Word and the administration of his sacraments, the means of grace. We might assume, certainly, that the person who despises these means of grace has in fact signed his own death warrant, spiritually speaking. We may not assume, however, that the one who deems he will not benefit from the means of grace has in fact rejected them. A Christian who feels hopeless may simply have no comprehension of how the gospel may serve him in a given instance. A fellow believer may assure him that Christ's words of forgiveness are his great weapon against Satan. But he is unable to control his hopelessness. He concludes that there is no chance his weapon will work at this time.

Visualize a woman who is being stalked. After much deliberation, she purchases a gun, believing this man potentially could harm her. Then one day he forces himself into her apartment. Having heard some suspicious sounds outside the door, the woman has retrieved her gun and makes her way to the kitchen and the nearest phone where she can dial for help. But there stands her dreaded adversary. Instinctively she raises both hands and points her weapon at him. As she looks into his eyes, however, she is overcome by his voice. In a familiar overbearing tone, he rebukes her: "You don't have the courage! Put your gun down!" His demand is quite silly actually. She clearly has him outgunned. In one moment she could end his intimidating actions. But as he advances toward her, she remains in a frozen pose with her gun still pointing in the same direction. Having lost hope that she can stand up to him, she is simply unable to pull the trigger.

It can happen to the disturbed believer who gives up on life. He loses hope that God's Word will be of any service to him. God's message concerning forgiveness and salvation will have no effect against his inner accusations. To God he's a no-good. The Lord should not bother reaching out to him with his message of grace. He's not worthy of it! It is not that this weary believer has dropped his weapon. He is simply incapable of using it. In his distorted opinion, the "gun is empty." Inasmuch as he is unable to reflect on God's blessings, God's Word is wanting. It holds no meaning for him. All he can think about is why he is entitled to nothing from God and his neighbor but loathing and shunning.

This is not a deduction you should permit yourself to make: that if an individual is not hearing the gospel or applying it to his personal situation, this means he has rejected it. A great number of people with a wide variety of problems suffer from hopelessness. But this you may believe regarding the troubled believer who is hearing little or feeling little: in every instance the Lord will uphold his faith through the Word and sacraments.

Faith-sustaining Baptism

When suicide strikes a Christian home, people invariably try very hard to comfort the closest survivors. Some will state, "He was not in control of his faculties." Or it may be said in light of her tragic solution to her troubles, "That wasn't your daughter!" or "That wasn't the mother who raised you." Proving more beneficial over the long run and comforting to the surviving family are words about God's grace and Holy Baptism. As a sacrament of our Lord, Baptism has the power to save on a daily basis. The apostle Peter declares, "Baptism . . . now saves you" (1 Peter 3:21). To say it somewhat differently, the greatest source of strength following a suicide comes not from knowing that underneath all the anxiety and pain and perhaps delusional thinking, the suicide was still a good person. Families are consoled by the fact that God in his grace has accepted the sacrifice of his Son as a payment for every sin, including the sin of suicide. As surely as this Christian was baptized, we may believe that his sin could no longer disqualify him from God's kingdom. In Baptism, God personally pledged to furnish him with his grace and every blessing. And that is exactly what he did.

To be baptized is to enter a state of grace and benefit from God's ever-continuing promise to the believer.[1] St. Paul writes, "All of you who were baptized into Christ have clothed yourselves with Christ" (Galatians 3:27). In Baptism God puts Christ's name on you, thereby pledging to give you everything you require for your salvation including protection against the assaults of the devil, the world, and your flesh. You have put on Christ, and you still have him when your sin wages an offensive against your faith. Despite the fact that temptation never gives you a rest and you sin every day of your life, your baptism has the final word over sin. And the word is *Christ*. As surely as God sees your baptism, he sees Christ who covers up your sin.

Baptism defines the state of grace. Living under God's grace is not something that comes and goes depending on how ominous your most recent sin is. You have an ongoing relationship with God. By his grace, God wants you as an heir of his kingdom both in this life and the next. And through Holy Baptism, he makes it so. Despite your continuing efforts to go your own way, by your baptism God reels you in again and again.

Imagine it's like visiting with a friend while holding in your arms a child who is just a few months old. As the minutes go by, the child grows impatient. Soon he starts fidgeting with all his might trying to escape. The child does not want to be dropped. He just does not want to be held any longer. He has better things to do. And unfortunately as the child continues to squirm to free himself from your grip, you finally lose your hold and he slips through your arms.

A different story is told of God's children who are baptized, thereby receiving God's grace. God never drops us. In the state of grace, Christ lays hold of us more strongly than our faith lays hold of him.[2] In the end, nothing can pry us from his hand. "I give them eternal life," he assures us. "No one can snatch them out of my hand. My Father, who has given them to me, is greater than all; no once can snatch them out of my Father's hand" (John 10:28,29). There is no power in all creation that can loosen God's hold on us through his Word and rob us of our faith. There is no hardship, no sin, no disease, and no death that is stronger than God's grace.

"How can he be in heaven? He died because he committed suicide!" If it was another sin that precipitated a Christian's death, the question might not even be asked. A teenage girl goes parking with her boyfriend to take their relationship to the "next step." *Just then* a bolder slips off a ledge from the cliff above them and crushes the two. Did this young lady go to hell because in a moment of weakness she made a bad choice? An underage young man defies his parents' curfew. After having engaged in a drinking contest with a few buddies, he speeds back to his apartment. *Just then* he makes an unfortunate turn and wraps his car around a lamppost. Did he go to hell? A husband gets into an argument and swears at his wife, then decides to go for a walk. *Just then* he is struck by lightning. Did he go to hell? A grade-school student steals a basketball from the school gymnasium and runs home. *Just then* he slips on the ice, hits his head on the pavement, and never regains consciousness. Did he go to hell? A couple waiting for a taxi after a heavy rain are sprayed from top to bottom with gooey mud by a passing truck. Stepping out into the road, the man gives an obscene gesture as she yells a couple choice profanities. *Just then* they are both hit by a second truck. Did they both go to hell? Most of these stories might be considered absurd. Realistically, you would not expect this to happen to anyone you know, Christian or not. The odds are against it. Or it may be pointed out that in the instances cited, the deceased did not die by their own hands. They nevertheless did die having given in to the power of temptation in the last moments of their lives. Their sins in each instance proved fatal.

A Christian who dies is not to be classified under one of two groups: those who die in sin or those who die in faith. To believe in a state of grace is to believe in the power of Baptism. Forgiveness of every sin becomes your personal possession. This means Christ will cover your *final* sins with his blood. God saves you finally not because you leave this life having avoided in the last moments any sinful thoughts, desires, words, and deeds. He saves by his divine means, by which he gives you forgiveness and sustains your faith. He saves you by his gospel and Holy Baptism. "Repent and be baptized, every one of you," Peter declares, "in the name of Jesus Christ for the forgiveness of your sins" (Acts 2:38). It is for this reason that when a loved one dies by suicide, you may receive comfort knowing that he was baptized. For centuries the church allowed the sin of suicide to have the final say over God's Word. When *Christ* is given the final say, you are assured that the Christian is saved by God's grace, despite how tragic his sin, even if it is suicide.

By Chance or by God's Choice?

How can I be sure he's in heaven?

There are times in our lives when a given event seems to happen by fluke. That is how I would explain the most incredible thing I have ever witnessed. A number of years ago, my eldest son and I attended a Detroit Tiger's game. Peter, who was about nine years old at the time, decided to bring along his baseball glove with hopes of catching a foul ball. My reaction was predictable: "Yeah, sure. We'll see about that!" I didn't verbalize what I was thinking, but it was apparent to me that the chances of his actually ending up with a ball were less than remote. My thoughts changed, nevertheless, when at the bottom of the second inning, a foul ball was hit in the stands over our heads. At first it seemed to be another ball someone else would claim. But as luck would have it, that ball began to ricochet between the seats before making a sudden change in course. And that is when what I had previously deemed impossible occurred. The ball came bouncing back toward us, slid over my son's shoulder—and while he wasn't looking—rolled down his arm and into his glove! Not only had he made no effort to catch the ball, I actually had to inform him that the ball was in his glove. Once more my reaction was predictable: "I can't believe it! What are the chances of such a thing?! What are the odds?!"

125

Two possibilities exist with respect to someone going to heaven. It happens either by *chance*—we just so happen to find our way into God's good graces—or it is God's *choice* that saves us. Christ's church has always accepted the latter as true, referring to it as the doctrine of predestination. Before God even made the earth, he predestined us to heaven through the redeeming blood of his Son. We may therefore entrust our faith to his care and believe that nothing will happen to our faith. St. Paul assures us of this, saying, "He chose us in him before the creation of the world. . . . In *love* he predestined us" (Ephesians 1:4,5).

The basis of God's choosing you from eternity is his love for you. Some may wonder, though, whether this could prove to be a risky game for God. Can he really consider only his love in choosing us and not first determine how we might "pan out" as Christians. Consider a couple who agrees to adopt, having been frustrated for some time trying to conceive a child. Eventually they opt for adopting a "high risk" baby and soon bring home a child who has been born prematurely and whose mother was on drugs during her pregnancy. Some might ask, "Why not wait a little longer for a healthier child?" So many things could go wrong and all the love in the world will not avert the heartbreak they will face.

You similarly may ask whether it was wise for our Father to pledge in advance to adopt you and me for all eternity. So he loves us! How can he choose to save us before we are even brought into this world? What about the risks involved? Who is to say we will remain in the faith? Not only are we conceived in sin with predispositions for self-loathing, hopelessness, and despair. We're proud, unreasonable, and reckless. But the words of the apostle remain: "In love he predestined us to be adopted as his sons *through Jesus Christ*" (Ephesians 1:4,5).

It was more than loving sentiment that moved God to choose us as his very own. He so loved us that before time even began, he resolved that his Son would die for us. His love for you and me is such that he determined both to *give* us faith in his Son and to *preserve* our faith before he created the first blade of grass and flower of the field. The teaching of predestination assures us of our Father's decision to adopt us for all eternity despite our deficiencies. Despite his knowledge of our sin, he obligated himself before time even existed to care for us and sustain us as only our gracious Father can.

God's choice to save us is nothing less than his commitment to help us despite our spiritual deficiencies. This he promises through the words of the gospel, absolution, Baptism, and the Sacrament of the

Altar. God does not leave our destiny in heaven to chance. He did not create heaven only to let some fluke of nature decide whether or not we would ever get there. We need not fear that God's grace will in some way be compromised by our sin. Again St. Paul reassures us, saying, "In him we were also chosen, having been predestined according to the plan of him *who works out everything in conformity with the purpose of his will*" (Ephesians 1:11). If you trust in Christ as your Redeemer from sin, you can also trust that God has planned your future from the beginning of time and that eternal salvation is yours, not by chance but by God's choice.

That is finally why we can be sure a Christian who chose suicide is in heaven. Despite his sin that cost him his life, we can be sure he died a believer. God chose him long before his dear child became ill and long before he lost hope and opted to initiate his escape. Before this Christian was made a believer through the gospel, before he was baptized, before he was born, even before anyone was born, God chose him to enjoy the glories of the next life.

Conclusion

People will occasionally speculate about what might happen if an immovable object were to meet up with an irresistible force. Would one or the other yield under this new and unforeseen development? Would one or the other be overwhelmed, changed, or compromised? Naturally I am speaking of a paradox that is not genuine but make believe. Perhaps those who dreamed it up imagined that God is inadequate, that he did not cover all the bases when he created this universe. So much is "out of sync"! It is always difficult to determine where good ends and evil begins.

People also spend idle time speculating about what happens when the greatest blessing on earth encounters the worst burden. What happens when Christian faith chances upon human hopelessness? Does one or the other have to yield? The answer is no. The paradoxes pertaining to a Christian suicide are resolved in each case when we call to mind the grace of God. We come to terms with the suicide of a beloved parishioner or a Christian friend or a loved one when we know what Christ accomplished on the cross for every sinner. He guarantees his grace and salvation to all believers. And nothing can take that away from us, "neither death nor life, neither angels nor demons, neither the present nor the future, nor any powers, neither height nor depth, nor anything else in all creation" (Romans 8:38,39).

Notes

[1]David P. Scaer, *Baptism* (St. Louis: The Luther Academy, 1999), p. 14, quotes Leif Grane, *The Augsburg Confession,* translated by John H. Rasmussen (Minneapolis: Augsburg Publishing House, 1987), pp. 46,47.

[2]Martin Chemnitz, *The Lord's Supper,* translated by J. A .O. Preus (St. Louis: Concordia Publishing House, 1979), p. 193.

Part Four

Grieving Loved Ones Search for a Scapegoat

(As you read this section, you will note that I have composed my thoughts in the second person, as though I am writing directly to a grieving family. My hope is to provide the reader with some specific suggestions on how to minister to those grieving for a suicide.)

"What Were You Thinking?!"

Should I blame my husband?

The judgment is almost universal. Someone must be blamed for what has immobilized an entire family. But where do you begin? In more than just a few families, the deceased ends up being the first target of criticism. You fixate on the questions: "How could he do this?" "Didn't he give any thought to those he would leave behind?" The easiest way to deal with the suicide of a loved one is to judge your loved one and his sinful act in a way that you would never judge yourself. This family member was bitter at life and did not want to put up with life's troubles any longer. "What were you thinking?!" you protest. "I would never have done this to you!" Getting no response from the deceased, it is very easy to draw your conclusion: "What you did was cowardly, thoughtless, inexcusable! You were just thinking about yourself!" If you finally convince yourself that it's time to let him off the hook, your thoughts reorganize, provoking the same old questions: "Why?! What could you possibly hope to gain from this idiotic act?!"

Suicide is a sin that you want to forgive. But it is clear you will require some help to do so. It is always easier to judge than it is to forgive. It is easier to permit suicide's stigma to fester than to obtain an understanding concerning depression and other conditions that lead to a sense of hopelessness. Even so, getting an education in the causes of suicidal thinking will not aid the process of forgiving. You can forgive the one who hurt you, but not because you come to understand something about his burden. The ability to forgive is not achieved by trying to imagine the staggering pain your loved one sustained. You forgive not inasmuch as you have worked through your grief or have perceived that your life is back on track. Forgiving is possible in every case only when you believe in the forgiveness your Savior earned for you by his ransoming death on a cross. Christ gave his life for this person who, like you, was a sinner from birth. And now you have the privilege to forgive "not seven times, but seventy-seven times" (Matthew 18:22).

"His Wife Drove Him to It!"

Outside judging

Understanding and support are crucial at this time. Sadly, it is also a time when ignorance and blame take center stage. In the aftermath of a suicide, it may seem commonplace. Friends abandon those they love. Instead of recognizing the devastating event as an opportunity to reach out to those who are especially hurting, people point fingers. In their opinion, there is only one way to make sense of the matter. The situation at home was beyond intolerable. Someone proved to be an unbelievable burden and drove this loved one over the edge.

Today's enduring stigma about suicide, as I have indicated, has much to do with the general population's inadequate understanding of depression. People are not informed about depression and its strong link to the sense of hopelessness. Nor do they grasp how this same hopelessness is linked to suicide. They learn about this horrible and apparently unspeakable event, and they want to understand. Their first reaction, unfortunately, is to presume that one of the survivors should be held responsible. My suggestion to the family is to give people a chance to hear your perspective on things. Let them understand something about depression and hopelessness and your family's loss. Yes, some will continue their gossiping. People whom you love may even sever their ties with you. I can recall more than one couple in my parish who quit the congregation following my wife's suicide. Others, however, and perhaps those from whom I would not have expected it proved themselves the truest of friends. I am sure you will experience the same thing. People will suddenly surface who wish to learn from your perseverance. They will not need to be taught how to explain things in a more positive context. Standing by you, they realize that love "always protects, always trusts, always hopes, always perseveres" (1 Corinthians 13:7).

 A real Christian will flee evil desires (2 Timothy 2:22). Yet this Christian could not restrain himself from taking his own life.

Inside judging

If the suicide of a Christian is a paradox, it is a paradox that those outside the circle of loved ones are not required to resolve, at least not to any degree of satisfaction. They have sided with a majority who have ruled that normal people do not despair. "People like you and me would never consider taking their own lives." If most people think the guy down the street killed himself because he was copping out on life or came from a dysfunctional family, you and I might draw the same conclusion.

When, on the other hand, it is a member of the family or someone very close to you who has committed suicide, you probably will not side with popular opinion. More likely, you will give the matter some independent and painstaking thought. You will want to understand what others are not willing to understand. You may even agonize over it as you search for someone to whom you may attribute blame.

If I am describing you at this time, I encourage you to keep in mind what is behind suicide's stigma. It is caused by ignorance. For whatever reason, people have remained uninformed about the hopelessness that precedes suicide. Understand also that the family of a suicide too may be affected by the stigma of a suicide. Members of the family may draw similar conclusions about why this death has occurred, as do those outside the home. They imagine that something was seriously wrong with the individual or with someone in the household. Either they committed a horrible sin, which the rest of the family would never consider doing, or someone within their family circle was causing them incredible stress.

Christians through the years have believed they have only two choices when it comes to reacting to a suicide. Either you point the finger, laying blame upon one or more of the survivors, or you concede that this loved one was not a Christian when he died. He fell away, giving up his faith. Typically, it is easier to find fault with someone other than this dear loved one who is now gone.

Should I blame someone in my family?

It is a temptation I fought more than I care to mention, thinking back and analyzing how a certain individual may have contributed to Jean's mode of thinking and her attitude toward life. I needed my target. Who influenced her most unfavorably over the years? Who helped her adopt unrealistic expectations with respect to her future? Who discouraged her when she needed encouragement?

Eventually I took aim at Jean's father. Jean had shared with me that his behavior at times had been somewhat controlling while she was growing up. On the one hand, he allowed no opportunity for the family to question a decision of his. On the other hand, when others did take him on, he would keep his emotions and resentments bottled up. It became a tool for dealing with the family. Apparently he would go hours or even days without talking as a way of communicating that you—as a member of the family—had crossed the line.

In my idle speculation, I determined, on the basis of this environment, that Jean had learned to internalize her troubles. If her father had spoken his mind, she would have learned to do the same. Hence, when things got bad and life seemed beyond repair, she would not have been so lacking in her coping skills. But I eventually gave up my conjecturing when I came to know more about depression and how it had surely affected her.

The question is, How did things get so out of control? Members of the family will start blaming one another when they lack an adequate understanding of the nature or magnitude of their loved one's hopelessness. All they know is that this daughter, father, sister, or husband gave up. But why did he or she give up? What is the alternative to concluding that something happened to this person's faith? In order to make the case that this much-loved individual died a Christian, you look for a scapegoat. You assert that a parent or spouse, whatever the case may be, was a scourge or a cross in the deceased's life and drove him one step too far. If it is a matter of choosing blame for yourself or someone else, you may choose that other person in the house. It is your opinion that this relative affected your loved one in an extremely devastating manner. Or this person failed to have the positive effect he or she should have.

When family blame goes unuttered and unchallenged, speculation begins breeding in every corner of the home. "So-and-so didn't spend sufficient time being a mom or dad to her. That's why she killed herself!" Or "It was her husband, what's-his-name, who had to work all that overtime and just wasn't there for her." "Had he or she only been a better listener and tried to understand what was out of sync, things would never have deteriorated to the degree they did." At a time when families need to share their grief and offer one another encouragement, they unfortunately become involved in a bitter game of projecting blame to the nearest target where it might stick.

The blame game is commonplace among family members following a suicide. The ultimate result, however, is that no one receives the support that's so desperately needed. Healing is stunted and any form of recovery is out of reach. The blame game obviously can appear in various forms. Blaming need not consist of audible words in every case. Surviving family members engage in an unfortunate game we might call "the silent treatment." The idea is, if you cannot shut people up, you can shut them out and prevent them from interacting with you. And you may become quite successful at it. Don't talk. Don't touch. Grieve alone.[1] Of course, it does not help the family. Instead, misconceptions and wrong information are allowed to flourish, while guilt and anger rage on quietly.[2] There is an alternative to permitting such anger and hurt to fester in your home. Recall as a family how Christ removed the blame of every sinner when he gave up his life for us. Remember your opportunity to pray, "Forgive us our debts, as we also have forgiven our debtors" (Matthew 6:12).

Can I blame the doctor or hospital?

Hindsight is always 20/20. Looking back you can see very clearly what should have been done or, I should say, what you believe should have been done. This explains the resentments I nurtured for a time against those from whom Jean had received professional help. Why couldn't they be straight with me regarding Jean's depression and how serious her condition had become? I certainly was not getting any useful information from Jean! In her somber silence, she offered no indication whether her condition was improving or deteriorating. Why didn't the psychiatrist warn me things might take a tragic turn and say more to alert me? Why did the visiting nurse remark that Jean was looking better and suggest she was doing so well under the latest medication? Jean knew better, as she later related to me, reinforcing my own doubts. But I felt obligated to accept the words of the nurse. She was, after all, the expert. Thinking back, I am sure Jean was plotting her final departure the very time this professional made her last visit! On the day Jean took her life, I now know she should not have been at home but in the hospital.

For other grieving families, it may have been evident that their loved one should not have been released from the hospital when he was. It later became clear that this family member was not out of danger but was still suicidal. Survivors, in such cases, may complain about the psychiatric ward whose staff failed to remain abreast of their loved one's state. Keep in mind, however, that patients in a mental health facility often learn quickly what things they ought not to say if they want to be discharged or let out on a pass. If they are desperate to get out, their only chance may be to con those standing in their way. Rule number one: Do not verbalize your suicidal thoughts or desires. To be sure, those serving the mentally ill and severely depressed in hospitals are trained to identify manipulative behavior. Unfortunately, no one is immune to making an occasional wrong decision with respect to who is ready to go home and who ought to remain under hospital care.

Survivors will often fault the hospital or a psychiatrist for the suicide. The staff was remiss in diagnosing their loved one's condition and how severe it had become. Families may also blame those in charge for failing to prescribe the right medication. The doctor should have anticipated that the medication would not work in this case. The prescription or dosage should have been changed a long time ago. Or perhaps the physician did change the medication, but that's when all hell broke loose. The loved one sank into a deeper depression from which he never recovered. On the other hand, maybe his depression was lifted somewhat, but this only emboldened him to act on what he had been contemplating for some time. In either case, a short time later, your loved one committed suicide.

Many tragic stories could be told concerning those who never acquired the right medication. This does not mean, however, that a given psychiatrist was not doing his job. A given doctor cannot know any more about a loved one's condition than what he comes to understand through the science of medicine. This is true no matter what the patient's condition. We may choose to trust our doctor's expertise or choose not to. However, if we *do* accept his help, our consent does not make him omniscient or infallible. He could make a career out of treating your husband or mother or child and still be ignorant regarding what ultimately might trigger a suicide attempt. Neither medication nor counseling proves absolutely reliable in every case.

Whether we attempt to assign blame for a given suicide to a doctor or to the closest family members, we are not resolving the paradox of a Christian's suicide. We are merely failing to address the unsettling truth that Christian families are not immune to mental illness and someone becoming suicidal. How do we explain why *this* Christian desired to end his life? Unless we look beyond chemical and hereditary issues and the family environment, the stigma affiliated with a Christian's suicide can only persist.

Keep in mind that it is sometimes easier to blame the world than to fault one individual. Perhaps it is very evident to us that people should know more and care more about the depressed and suicidal individuals. Society ought to be more in tune with issues pertaining to suicide and develop more effective ways to prevent such disasters to the family. Whether we blame just one or a million, however, holding others responsible will not help us cope with our loss. Somehow we must receive our help from Christ. As the Lamb of God, who takes away the sin of the world (John 1:29), he is the one scapegoat to whom we can turn for forgiveness with regard to our *own* sin and to find closure with regard to *another's* sin.

"God Gave Him More Than He Could Handle!"

If suicide survivors were capable, they would prefer to grieve as others do who deal with the sudden death of a loved one. When a family member dies of a heart attack or a ruptured aneurysm, mourners do not usually spend as much time pointing fingers and laying blame. There is a medical explanation, and most families in time will accept it. How nice it would be if we could simply accept the fact that this daughter or son, this husband or wife, this father or mother suffered from a severe case of depression and eventually he or she died. The loved one became subjected to an overwhelming sense of hopelessness. Life's alterations were too abrupt, drove this person to a point of despair, and the rest is history. It is not our nature, however, to accept suicide as a cause of death. For one thing, suicide is irrational. For another thing, our family member was not acting in a normal manner *before* he took his life. We conclude that there is another deeper explanation. Someone must be held responsible for his death.

If your loved one died before all members in the family had a chance to educate themselves about depression and other depressive disorders, you probably have spent some time blaming one another for his suicide. If your loved one struggled for some years, however, your family's initial response might have been to blame God. What God permits us to suffer is often more than we desire or believe we are capable of suffering. When we lose sight of this fact, we tend to hold our Lord accountable for our trials, the trials of others, and whether or not we are able to deal with them. The paradox concerning our loved one's suicide, in our opinion, is God's fault.

Did God give him too much?

Christians frequently state that God will not give us more than we can handle. I assume they are attempting to interpret 1 Corinthians 10:13, where the apostle declares, "God is faithful; he will not let you be tempted beyond what you can bear." This passage is very comforting for the believer who is given various crosses to bear during his life. God will not test or chasten us over and above what we are capable of enduring. But there is a crucial question that deserves our attention here. Is Paul referring to what our bodies are given to bear or what our faith is given to bear? Most people fail to make a distinction between the two. As a result, another paradox is observed with respect to the Christian who commits suicide.

God doesn't give us more than we can handle. Yet this Christian we knew could not cope with life and consequently ended his life.

Observing a paradox in this situation is unfortunate. If we were to imagine that God will never give us more than we can handle physically, emotionally, or psychologically, what shall we conclude about the person who is overwhelmed in any given case and can no longer function as he has in the past? He has a nervous breakdown. He has a post-traumatic stress disorder following a catastrophic life event. He is overcome by severe depression. Has he lost his faith? Or did God merely give him more than he could handle psychologically? What shall we conclude about the person who has developed an extreme case of Parkinson's or Alzheimer's disease that proves to be more than he can handle from a physical standpoint? Is God going back on his word? Obviously not.

The correct understanding of 1 Corinthians 10:13 is that the Lord will not give our *faith* more than our *faith* can handle. It is, after all, the Lord who is the author and perfecter of our faith (Hebrews 12:2). If it appears, therefore, that God has given us too much for our health, we cannot assume he is given us too much from a spiritual standpoint. Rather, when we encounter temptation, God always provides a way out so that we can stand up under our temptation (1 Corinthians 10:13). Despite what trials God has allocated to us, through his Word he both works and sustains in us faith in our Savior.

This is not to say, however, that God will not permit a Christian to be tempted. He may permit a believer to struggle in his faith, what Luther referred to as *Anfechtung*. God may permit him to become vulnerable to attack by the devil, the world, and his own sinful nature. A severe case of depression, as an example, may tempt the believer to despair. God allows a person to inherit a predisposition for depression, knowing full well that he will not handle things when they come to a head. But God does not give a Christian too much. God does not kick us who believe in Christ when we are down. He does not permit a Christian's depression, which attacks his ability to reflect in a normal way on the gospel's blessings, to snatch away his faith. The Lord remains at work through his Word and never abandons a believer to the effects of his disease. Isaiah prophesied about the Christ, "A bruised reed he will not break, and a smoldering wick he will not snuff out" (Isaiah 42:3). God will never permit life's random circumstances to drive us, his children, away from him. It simply is not possible for incidents of this kind to occur, because they are never a part of God's will.

Was this really God's will?

As I look back on Jean's disease, I now realize my children and I were bearing the burden of our dear loved one but were not capable of understanding it. Our wife and mom was preparing to die, but we were not permitted to help her.

Loved ones and friends may try to comfort you with a loving reminder that, however horrifying the death of your loved one may have been, it was God's will! But frankly, you are not finding their words very encouraging. Who do they think they are with their pious remarks, asserting that you who mourn must accept God's will? All you have been able to do so far is question: "Why *my* husband? *my* mother? *my* son? Why *my* family?"

It is commonly accepted that no one can anticipate God's will with respect to one's future. At the same time, a good Christian is instructed to *accept* God's will, whether he is capable of understanding it or not. These two givens may pose little trouble for us as long as life's circumstances go our way. Something else occurs to us, however, when life does its number on us. "Why *should* I accept God's will? I cannot comprehend it looking ahead! I cannot comprehend it looking back! Why must I acknowledge that because something is God's will, it must also be beneficial?" We take one quick look at our lives and protest, "*This* is good?"

People who expect us to conform to a certain way of thinking, giving us little or no reason for doing so, we regard as unreasonable. Sometimes we feel the same way about God. When we are given no choice but to go along with that which makes no sense, we resent it. Events that simply disrupt our comfortable lives—possibly bringing us heartache—often trigger anger and hurt. "How could you do this, God?" we object.

You may have no concerns about God's will as it relates to his sovereignty. You are confident he can care for every one of his creatures. David rightly declared, "The eyes of all look to you, and you give them their food at the proper time. You open your hand and satisfy the desires of every living thing" (Psalm 145:15,16). Your problem is that you do not always see your Lord at work. You do not see him opening his hand and satisfying all who look to him. What you observe, in fact, may be the very opposite of what you desire. Why? It is not that God has reneged on his promise to provide. Rather, your perception of his continuing care has been impaired.

Understand that everything you see in God's creation is affected by the dominance of sin on this earth and the fact that God's perfect creation has been altered by sin. Sin imposes upon your life every kind of trial, suffering, and tragedy. But this does not mean sin has rendered God less powerful. Sin does not change God's resolve to care for you. Neither can sin alter the particulars of God's will and *how* he will bless you in this life.

The difficult thing for you about God's will is that it may seem theoretical at best. If so, you need to hear of him who is the heart and center of Scripture and give ear to God's will concerning his Son. Initially, the tragedy associated with Christ's crucifixion is inconceivable in the mind of us sinners. Was this God's will? Here pinned to that God-forsaken cross is one man, and yet he's suffering for the sins of all mankind. He is experiencing the most brutal form of execution ever contrived by the human mind; cold spikes connecting his flesh to wooden beams like some cutout pinned to a bulletin board. He is loaded with every sin of every sinner and faces God's judgment for it all. We truly have no comprehension of the depths of Christ's suffering. And yet perhaps there is something even more difficult for us to understand. This is our perfect God suffering this cruel punishment for our sin! God is holy! He cannot be punished! Yet God the Father would see to it that God the Son *was* punished. The Son, who is no less righteous or holy than his Father, is abandoned by his Father to these wicked bloodthirsty savages. God is apparently going against what it means to be God.

For the suicide survivor, God's will may seem like a horrible paradox. How can this be God's will? My loved one was a Christian! How can I recognize this tragic death as something good? You may silence such questions by placing the focus on your Savior. Was the cross of Christ a good thing? Obviously we do not judge whether there was some benefit in Christ's bloody crucifixion by determining whether or not the circumstances leading up to it were just. We give thought, rather, to what we know about God's will. The prophet Isaiah asserts, "It was the LORD's will to crush him and cause him to suffer" (Isaiah 53:10). Christ's suffering seems to be a terrible and horrifying contradiction. However, we resolve that apparent contradiction by remembering that Jesus was suffering in our place as our substitute. Our Lord Jesus Christ became the object of God's punishment for our sin in order to prevent our sin from having the last say in our lives. Despite what I might tell you about Jean's death or what you might have to say about the death of your loved one, the bottom line is very simple. Christ died what was perceived to be a tragic death to end all other tragic deaths.

As you try to make sense out of your painful loss, the will of God will to some extent remain hidden from you. This is not to say, however, that you cannot accept his will or benefit from it. The will of God shall always comfort, insofar as we know God as our gracious Father. We recognize that he sent his only-begotten Son that we might be forgiven of all sin and guaranteed every blessing essential for this life. "For my Father's will is that everyone who looks to the Son and believes in him shall have eternal life, and I will raise him up at the last day" (John 6:40). When we believe this, we can put our burden into his hands—even when we are met with tragedy—and be relieved in time of all anger and grief.

Was God making the best of a bad situation?

This question may represent the cry of any number of suicide survivors who in their shock and grief are trying to make sense of their shared tragedy. "Can we conclude that God saw his child suffering terribly under depression, etc., and offered relief? Might he have seen how the family was bearing a tremendous burden and determined to spare them further grief? Or with regard to an even more somber situation, did God determine that depression would drive this child of his away from his Word, causing him to lose his faith? As horrible and tragic as suicide is, did God possibly conclude that suicide was a better outcome than permitting things to continue as they were, letting a fragile situation deteriorate into something far worse and from which there would be no means of repairing things?"

Some survivors speculate that suicide was God's merciful alternative to seeing their loved one eventually fall away. I have had this implied to me more than once—that God permitted Jean's catastrophe so that he might salvage what was left of her faith.

Speculating regarding God's judgments is never helpful. Moses gave this word to the Israelites: "The secret things belong to the LORD our God, but the things revealed belong to us and to our children forever" (Deuteronomy 29:29). It is not unusual to have a pressing question in life remain unanswered despite your great yearning for God to shed some light on the matter. This does not mean that God leaves us in the dark concerning what we need to know as his children. What you need to know, as indicated by the apostle, is that "in *all things* God works for the good of those who love him" (Romans 8:28). There are no exceptions to God's decree. Everything that takes place during the entire history of the world, good or bad, will serve for the good of those whom God has elected to spend eternity with him. In other words, God does not determine as he goes along what he will do to assist us spiritually. God is not to be likened to a professional firefighter, making his constant rounds about the earth, "putting out fires" set by Satan and the devil's cohorts. The Lord has not revealed himself in Scripture as our "fix-it God," who is obligated on occasion to "backpedal" whenever he observes some development in our lives that might trouble our faith. This is particularly relevant with respect to one's faith in Christ. We may never conclude that under certain unhappy circumstances, God's Word lacks the power essential for sustaining the faith of a given believer and that he therefore must resort to "Plan B."

The real point is, God never abandons his children. For the sake of your faith, God never allows you to suffer unsupervised miseries in life. Christ suffered according to God's will so that you might never be left to the mercy of your sin, to death, and to the devil. The question is not whether God could have prevented this tragedy. The question is whether any given death may occur apart from God's will. The answer is no. Our Lord declares in Deuteronomy, "See now that I myself am He! There is no god besides me. I put to death and I bring to life, I have wounded and I will heal, and no one can deliver out of my hand" (32:39). God is not speaking specifically in this passage to murder or suicide, but to all deaths. His words serve as a statement of fact, what you would know about God. However death occurs, it never takes place outside of God's will.

To say nothing about what you are able to understand, God works things for your good although you are undeserving of his goodness. Moreover, what you *can* understand and believe about our God is that he does not deliver loved ones from this world to deprive you and your family of essential love and support. He takes them home to rescue them from the sorrow and evil issued by the world and to give them instead the everlasting joys and glories promised by our Savior. Isaiah helps us put things in the right perspective: "The righteous perish, and no one ponders it in his heart; devout men are taken away, and no one understands that the righteous are taken away to be spared from evil" (57:1).

God does not have to make the best of a situation that has suddenly gone bad. By his infinite wisdom and grace—so that he might bless us in all things—he anticipates evil. From eternity God has determined how he will dominate Satan's efforts to overcome believers. It is why the Son of God would enter his own creation in order to die. Our Lord Jesus did not give up his spirit because he found himself trapped in the wrong place at the wrong time in a world gone mad. The Son of God died because he *willed* to die. According to the will of his Father, he died to atone for the sins of the whole world. He died so that our death might be swallowed up in victory (1 Corinthians 15:54).

It stands to reason, if God could use the inhuman behavior of those who fastened his own Son to a cross to save us eternally, he can use *today's* evil for our good. God can even use the objectives and ways of Satan to accomplish his purpose. Thus can we find comfort and strength in the case of the Christian who has died by the tragedy of suicide. Your loved one died not because God said "okay" to some warped thought which inadvertently entered that person's troubled mind. Your loved one died because, according to his merciful wisdom, our God and Savior deemed it was *time* for him to die.

A final question concerning God's will may be articulated by your pastor and others serving in the church. If we say this event took place in accordance with God's will, are we not also saying that God gave his approval to this Christian's suicide? God never in any way approves of sin. He opposes sin under every circumstance, hating all who do wrong (Psalm 5:5). Even so, God has the power to use sin to achieve his gracious purpose. The timing of death is God's will, not the wickedness or tragedy that makes some deaths so awful. The Lord, to be sure, may call a Christian home in another manner besides suicide in order to end his inner battle. But Christ chose to use the devil's efforts to terrorize you as a survivor to demonstrate his care, his compassion, and his power. Satan intended to harm you and me through the horrifying death of our loved ones, but God intended it for good (Genesis 50:20).

"It's All My Fault!"

Is it my fault she died?

It took me little time following Jean's suicide to recognize why she was taken to heaven. It was not because God wanted to rob me of a long and happy marriage with my loving wife. For reasons that would remain unknown to me, he determined that Jean should be in on the magnificent blessings of heaven earlier than I. But I soon realized that simply talking about God's will would not provide a satisfactory explanation of why she lost her life. I was convinced I had played a role in her death. I had failed her when she depended on me the most.

I was simply being logical. Why blame my wife, my father-in-law, or her doctor? I was much closer to the situation than they were. And why blame God, unless of course, I wished to reject what I have always believed about my Savior and his mercy. It was much easier to blame myself. I could make quite a case against myself, after all. And no one would argue with me since they were not privy to my judgments. I would not even find a Bible passage refuting my claim: "I'm the guilty one. It's all my fault she died!"

You may have little difficulty following the argument cited above. Living and suffering under guilt seems reasonable. If so, you must know you are not alone. Intense guilt among survivors of a suicide is widespread, if not universal. Perhaps you are feeling overwhelmed as you piece together what you believe precipitated this event. Your recollections are bent on convicting you of negligent behavior. You are convinced that what you should or should not have done prior to your love one's death will pester you for some time, perhaps for the rest of your life.

But it is normal, quite frankly, for *anyone* to place blame upon himself after losing a family member. It may make little difference as to how this loved one has died. People blame themselves when their spouse dies from a form of cancer that has gone undetected. They blame themselves when their child is killed in a car accident that presumably may have been prevented had this young person not volunteered to be the driver. In most cases, such people eventually will be talked out of their self-blame.

Grieving for a suicide, however, by definition is a different experience. As a mourner, you seem to have a choice. Blame the departed, blame God, or blame yourself. And maybe you do not want to blame the deceased or God anymore. Essentially, that is where I found myself. I remember what I told a brother of mine who attempted to persuade me that it was not rational for me to be blaming myself. There was no way that anyone would ever convince me that I was not responsible for Jean's death. I knew for a fact that I would feel guilty for the rest of my life.

Why such extreme guilt?

You may call it an unrelenting form of guilt, because there is no one else you can hold responsible for your loss. If you cannot pin the death on others or on God, what other possibility is there? It seems only reasonable, that *someone* be blamed. This was not a natural death. If you are honest with yourself, you'll learn something about your current grief. It is easier to get lost in your guilt and feel sorry for yourself than to resolve suicide's great paradox.

Survivor depression

Blame that is not silenced in time can generate depression. I still have periodic thoughts that maintain: "I sure was a lousy husband if she had to resort to this!" and "The grief I caused her must have been pretty awful if this was the best way of finding relief." Some survivors may even feel that they do not deserve to be loved. People deserve better than their pitiful efforts to serve. They may even believe they deserve to die. Perhaps you are feeling something more than mere grief and pain from your loss. It would not be unusual at this time, in fact, if you were experiencing a moderate form of depression.

If you are feeling depressed at this time, be assured that this is a common reaction for those attempting to cope with the death of a loved one. It is normal to question whether you could have done more as a father or mother, husband or wife, son or daughter. As a survivor, you may cross-examine yourself on all sorts of things, including whether you were worthy of his or her love. It is not appropriate, however, to feel guilty out of obligation to your loved one. Grieving is not the same as loving. Nor will grieving change the facts that led up to your family member's death and whether you ought to be exonerated or not.

For some time you may reserve the right to blame. Perhaps you find this preferable to having *others* judge you. What is more, depression or sincere grieving may become your proof to these others that you cannot be blamed for your loved one's death. If this is the case, I may ask you what difference does it make what others think if in the end *you* are still condemning yourself. If it is your desire to be the final judge in this matter, you have slipped into a common trap of suicide survivors. Having ruled out everyone else as the guilty party, you are left with all fingers pointing at yourself when in fact you are no more responsible for the suicide than any other survivor.

Instead of worrying how *others* may evaluate your guilt, you would be better served pondering what *God* makes of your guilt. Your gracious Father does not want you feeling depressed anymore than he desires it for that person who has been diagnosed with a severe case of clinical depression. If you are feeling an obligation to blame yourself for your family's great loss, remember that God has obligated himself to relieving you of blame. In the words of his apostle: "This then is how . . . we set our hearts at rest in his presence whenever our hearts condemn us. For God is greater than our hearts, and he knows everything" (1 John 3:19,20).

No one to talk to

Oftentimes a surviving family member will fail to consider how other members of the family experience very similar forms of guilt. It is because they are not talking to one another. As a family, they may have a nonverbal consensus that they will place the blame for their loved one's death on others outside the household. It was the mother who abused him, the boss who overworked him, the friend who got him in with the wrong crowd and into drugs, etc. However, if as individuals they are unsuccessful in diverting the blame away from themselves, they may find that they cannot talk to *anyone* about it. In which case they become stuck in their grief.

Perhaps you have experienced this to a degree. You would have preferred not to blame yourself. But you are thinking, "All I have to do is look at the evidence!" Even if there are no compelling facts to suggest that you be blamed, your conscience may just dig deeper. It may be intent not to lose in this matter. Assuming you have no answer to the ongoing indictments from within, your conscience may cause you to feel very alone. In order to be objective about any so-called damning evidence, however, and whether you might be blamed for the suicide, you need to talk to the other members of your family.

Hiding the facts

But maybe you are not convinced talking is always the answer. You'll grant that talking can be therapeutic. You are afraid, however, that those you love will just condemn you for your selfish ways and for failing to observe what was going on in your loved one's life. Or worse, they'll condemn your loved one. It is not uncommon for suicide survivors to hide the truth both from those outside their close circle of trusted loved ones and from their family and dearest friends. They often prefer mourning alone, afraid to seek comfort even from those closest to them. After all, they might inadvertently let some incriminating tidbit "out of the bag."

Does this sound familiar? You have believed if you say as little as possible, those whom you love will put the best construction on things. Or maybe they won't. They may speculate even more. And herein lies the problem. Even if you eventually silence people's speculations that you are to blame somehow, you may not be able to silence that *inner* voice, which issues a much different verdict.

Just imagine now if each member of your family is doing the same thing without realizing it. It explains why sometimes an entire family may be involved in a type of conspiracy to hide the facts of their loved one's death. They may, for example, try to con others into believing it was an unfortunate accident. Only then will they feel comfortable telling others about the death.

However, survivors who are unwilling to speak openly about the suicide and the guilt they feel only deprive themselves of the blessings of God's Word. Inasmuch as you do not permit others to speak Christ's message of forgiveness to you, you will not benefit from his message. Expressing your guilt and hearing Jesus' words of pardon are fundamental to Christian family living. James urges you, saying, "Therefore confess your sins to each other and pray for each other so that you may be healed" (5:16). Your Lord wants you to confess your sin regularly and to hear from fellow believers his forgiving gospel. Even if you do not always do a perfect job identifying the sin in your life, you may still confess your sin and believe that Christ's blood has removed it from God's sight.

Even so, you may argue that there is the matter of your family and what *they* are thinking. "But what will everyone say? We cannot tell people he committed *suicide.*" Your family perceives his suicide as a shameful secret that mustn't be leaked. Somehow you must protect his memory, not to mention your family's good name. Perhaps you disagree with your family. You are uncomfortable trying to hide the fact that he committed suicide. But you love your family and want to respect what pleases them.

Understand that a family's conspiracy of silence may simply lead from one lie to another. To keep quiet the truth about the suicide, you may also be forced to keep quiet the fact that your loved one was troubled before he died. You fail to mention that he was suffering from depression. Or you choose to remain silent about stormy relationships within the family. You fail to share with acquaintances that recent disruption in the home or what had overwhelmed your family member. To be sure, a few family secrets may be thought of as reasonable. It is privileged information. A multitude of secrets, however, may severely hamper honest and sincere interaction with others.

A considerable number of suicide survivors have difficulty being honest with friends about the death of their loved one. Unfortunately, this only hurts them, because the survivor is always left to wonder, do these friends know, and if so, how much? Not knowing whether others know, moreover, only restrains them from working through their grief and adjusting to their loss. This naturally leads to isolation and loneliness.[3] Meanwhile, the family is unable to escape the evidence. The death was still a suicide.

If you have not been able to make sense of your family's suicide, you need to know that you still have an opportunity to talk to each other about what you do know. Confess your sin to one another. Did you contribute to your loved one's sense of desperation? In what way do you feel responsible? You do not have to tell the world. But you certainly can tell each other. Then confess your faith to one another. Remind each member of your family that "[God] is faithful and just and will forgive us our sins and purify us from all unrighteousness" (1 John 1:9).

Justified grief

When Jean was suffering from major depression, I remember feeling hurt and even angry. Despite my best efforts, I was not able to please her. At the time, I was not linking her unreasonable wants and demands to her illness. After she died, I then felt an incredible sense of relief. The relief, however, came with a price.

If you are wondering why your guilt is sticking around, it may have something to do with the nature of your grief. You are experiencing a mixture of grief and relief. You are relieved that the burden you shared with your loved one is now gone. A very stressful and draining experience is finally behind you. It is not easy, after all, living with a depressed person, and it is even more difficult living with one who you know is suicidal. And that is why you are experiencing guilt. You have been relieved of this hardship and are ashamed to admit the relief you are feeling. But feeling shame because a cross has suddenly been lifted serves no purpose. Your sense of relief is natural to the recovery you can expect over the next several months. It is God's way. "He heals the brokenhearted and binds up their wounds" (Psalm 147:3).

Understanding what is behind your guilt and being rid of it is not the same thing. To the contrary, it is easy to obsess over what might have been. You may call it a self-indictment, and I am convinced everyone utters it who has been directly affected by a suicide. "If I had only . . . !" If I had only anticipated this desperate act! If I had only acted sooner. My indictment sounded something like this:

If only I had checked on Jean one more time before heading to my office. If only I had told her, that last morning, how much I loved her and given her a hug. If only I had insisted that she receive more counseling. If only I had talked to her about changing her psychiatrist! If only I had helped more around the home! If only I had spent more time with the children, offered to assist with all the chasing Jean was doing, and helped with keeping the house in order. If only I had not spent so many days working such long hours. If only I had helped her manage her daily schedule.

But I did not. And for some time I believed I was destined to spend the rest of life revisiting the days and hours just prior to Jean's death.

How do I get past the nagging "If I had only..."?

It is true both you and I *could* have done many things. In addition to what I have already mentioned, I could have quit work in order to "really be there" for Jean at every single instant. I could have been more loving and encouraging in both my actions and my words. I could have been more consistent, assuring her of my love and how she was so cherished by the family. Perhaps had I done all those things and God had still taken her home, I would be feeling a little more forgiven right now, or maybe not. Had I "been there" in one case, another situation would have probably popped up somewhere else. More than likely, it would have been just a matter of time before I found another way of putting myself on trial.

There are innumerable things we may choose to do or not to do to soothe a suffering loved one. Oftentimes, unfortunately, we simply do not think of them. Shall we be condemned for lacking common sense? That obviously would not be reasonable. Any Christian can play a role that has an inadvertent effect on conditions in the home. Any one of us might become involved in a type of sinful behavior that arguably could aggravate the depressed's sense of hopelessness. You or I may set up any number of variables that gave this person a reason in his mind to end his life. But as we later look back on what might have contributed to a heightened level of stress in the home, it does not explain why a loved one actually placed the noose around his neck or took that overdose or pulled the trigger. And it certainly does not make you or me responsible for another person's suicide. Thousands of other families may undergo similar pressures and burdens, but they manage to pull through them. Their loved one is still with them today.

You might argue that had you known more about his depression, you would have known what he was thinking! Had you known of certain activities cropping up in his life outside of the home, you could have predicted what would happen next. However, maybe your loved one *wanted* to keep you in the dark. People who, despite their suicidal ideas, want to be stopped will give clear messages of their intent. Others who are convinced that suicide is the only solution to their problem will fool everyone.[4] Your loved one may have worked your ignorance for his own purposes. If so, it may have been next to impossible for you to know what he was truly feeling and thinking from one day to the next, least of all the day when he committed suicide.

Every professional counselor or licensed psychologist, I am sure, will tell you the same thing. You did not *cause* the suicide. It was your loved one who resolved to carry out his suicide. If after listening to common sense, however, you still cannot stop blaming yourself for the death of your family member or get past the suspicion that others are holding you accountable, you may find that your grieving process has stalled. What shall you do then? Some survivors decide that it is easier to live with their guilt than to attempt to quiet their consciences and that nagging question: Why did she do it? Why did he do it? It takes little effort to rationalize living with guilt when you cannot change the past. Grief's echo changes from "If I had only . . . !" to "He died because . . ." He died because I was too controlling, I did not demonstrate enough affection or offer assistance when it was needed so badly. It can all be traced back to my failed relationship, my laziness, my preoccupation with other interests, my selfish disposition.

To rationalize, however, may be very irrational. It is illogical to observe a cause and effect relationship between one person's undesirable behavior and another person's suicide. Let us consider the facts. Suicide survivors oftentimes conclude that there is no chance they did not cause the suicide. But upon what have they based their ruling? Have they spoken with their loved one and asked, "Why did you do it? Was it because of me that you took your life?" Obviously not. There may be multiple answers to why they did it. But knowing the real and entire truth is not possible. Perhaps, to a large extent, that is why you are not feeling forgiven right now. You are powerless to know the whole truth as to why your loved one committed suicide and even more powerless to change it.

Our Savior's cure for a guilty conscience

That is not to say, however, that you must remain in the dark concerning other more important truths as they pertain to the death of your family member. There is but one truth you will find reassuring at this time. I speak of the truth regarding God's grace. Even if you are correct in your assessment that you made it easier for your loved one to take his life, Christ the Lord died for you. At just the right time, when you and I both were still powerless, Christ died for the ungodly (Romans 5:6).

And now, at the *current* time, Christ offers relief for guilty consciences through his Word. He tells us, "Come to me, all you who are weary and burdened, and I will give you rest" (Matthew 11:28). The rest he provides is the only true and valid forgiveness of sins. By his atoning blood, he forgives you for everything you might have done that contributed to your loved one's suicide. He forgives you for not being as responsible as you might have been in managing the circumstances at home. He forgives you for being a sinner who will continue to miscalculate the weight of a given burden carried by one under your care. Yes, he forgives you for being who you really are.

You can be sure that thoughts concerning what you *could have done* will return periodically. I am still pestered by such thoughts, more than 17 years after Jean's death. I know how I could have prevented her death and know even better that I will never have the opportunity to go back to that date to alter what happened just before she died. And so I know that my guilt will return from time to time. There are times I am not going to feel very forgiven. In addition, I am sure I am speaking for many of you who are convinced your guilt will never go away. This is not to say, however, that you are not forgiven. Remember forgiveness is not something you may claim because you have fulfilled certain duties; you have been there for certain people and this makes you feel good about yourself. Forgiveness is something you are privileged to believe in since Christ did not leave one sin on the cross for your Father to scrutinize. This is the one message you can rely on in every case to soothe your guilty conscience. Remember that "as far as the east is from the west, so far has he removed our transgressions from us" (Psalm 103:12). How far is that? I am not sure we can truly comprehend it. How does one measure what has neither a starting point nor an end? I guess the extent to which our sins have been taken away is infinite in distance and therefore in effect.

Feeling forgiven is not as important as *being* forgiven and being assured of what Christ has done to forgive the sins of the world. That is why you may give up your finger pointing with the exception of your constant pointing to the sacrifice of your Savior. No, you cannot undo your history. But neither can you undo Christ's. Whatever role you may have played—great or small—which might be construed as having prompted this suicide, Christ died for you. You are forgiven. But do not simply take my word for it. Listen to Scripture's assurances. Remember the words of the psalmist: "If you, O LORD, kept a record of sins, O Lord, who could stand? But with you there is forgiveness" (Psalm 130:3,4). Remember the words of St. Paul, who declares that in Christ "we have redemption through his blood, the forgiveness of sins, in accordance with the riches of God's grace" (Ephesians 1:7). Remember the apostle's assurance that "God demonstrates his own love for us in this: While we were still sinners, Christ died for us" (Romans 5:8).

Notes

[1] Hewett, *After Suicide,* p. 57.
[2] Ibid.
[3] Ibid., p. 101.
[4] Smolin, *Healing After the Suicide of a Loved One,* p. 118.

Part Five

Gospel Relief for the Hopeless

(Especially for Pastors)

The Church's Historical Response: Terrify With the Law

For centuries the most effective religious deterrent to suicide was the church's emphasis on the fear of God, the devil, and damnation. I am sure many were dissuaded as a result from following through with a suicide plan. It is highly unlikely, nevertheless, that the church lessened the despair of those who had thoughts of suicide. Instead, church leaders contributed, no doubt, to a sense of hopelessness. There was no putting the best construction on the matter; no other conclusion the believing community might draw. Either this former member of the church was *insane* or he was in *hell*.

Today we are more informed about depression, but a similar attitude persists among many clergy. Church leaders frequently fail to separate illness from sin. It is supposed that if this person is truly Christian, he ought to be able to overcome the effects of his depression. "We don't want to suggest it's all right for Christians to think about suicide! To take the law into your own hands and kill a human being is wrong, whether it is another person or yourself. Therefore, we are compelled to speak of suicide as a sin." I will agree that we must call suicide what it is, namely, self-murder. Pastors should not avoid addressing the *sin* of suicide when speaking with someone who is threatening to take his life. However, the message of the law should not serve as the last word. In the final round, exercising empathy and compassion will prove more effective in preventing suicide. We need to place an emphasis on forgiveness in this life over judgment in the next life.

Even so, you may not be ready to concede in any open way that there is forgiveness for the suicide. You may agree that suicide is forgivable and that some people who take their lives are believers. But this begs some questions in your opinion: "What if I am concerned about stopping a potential suicide? Common sense will surely prohibit me from talking about forgiveness. Might I not justify threatening the suicidal with hell, if in the end I save a life? If I do not inform the suicidal that he can go to heaven if he chooses to end his life, what shall I tell him?"

Let me first propose what we do not say. We never endorse false doctrine, arguing that it may have a practical use. We may not consider as an alternative to a *dangerous truth,* an *accommodating untruth.* We might call this an attempt to literally "scare the hell out of" the would-be suicide, and, at best, it is a very questionable notion of prevention. "If we warn them that people who commit suicide are those who have rejected God's help and have lost their faith, we should be able to deter them from following through. If we tell them that murderers will not inherit the kingdom of God, perhaps we can prevent them from doing something everyone will regret." Perhaps. Or perhaps our attempt to treat the symptoms of the person's disease will effect no change. Perhaps talking to them about their faith will have no bearing upon their current state of mind and what they may be liable to do next. Perhaps our words will only aggravate their current self-loathing and sense of hopelessness, reinforcing the conclusion that suicide is the only answer. Perhaps there are no words of warning that could serve as a necessary deterrent against self-executed disaster. Perhaps their only hope is the gospel.

Never should we withhold the good news from people who are hurting with the understanding that they might otherwise abuse it. Let's say someone confesses to having committed adultery. You are not going to reason to yourself: "I'd better not say anything to him about the blood of Christ that purifies us from all unrighteousness (1 John 1:9). He might decide to slip back into the same sinful behavior and do it all over again." As surely as he needs to hear the law in its full sternness, so he needs to hear the gospel in its full sweetness.[1] This also goes for the hopeless and suicidal person. You do not withhold the gospel's comfort for fear that a person will follow through with what he has been contemplating. If a fellow Christian confesses to you that he has thought about taking his life, you assure him that he is forgiven of this sin too.

Naturally, we would never promote another extreme with respect to a person who expresses the desire to end his life. And that is to avoid confronting with the law. Everyone is a sinner, and therefore everyone needs to hear the law's accusations and threats. On the other hand, what I am saying will hopefully be viewed as common sense. God's Word will not heal cancer. It will not reverse heart disease. Nor can threatening a person with hell lift him out of a state of severe depression or squelch any sort of suicidal impulse. When those who are under our spiritual care become a danger to themselves or perhaps others, it is not time to preach a sermon. Our intention is to comfort people in their depressive state and offer relief to the hopeless. And so, under most circumstances, I would advise that we not speak with a suicidal person about either heaven *or* hell. This is not to say, however, that we cannot relate the gospel to him. Instead of focusing on the next life, if in fact that is what's on his mind, we would be well advised to focus on God's love and his intended blessings for today. Assure him that Christ has paid for every sin of his. If he is not able to stop thinking about what is surely evil from God's standpoint, that is not to say that God will write him off as one who has "crossed the line." "If you, O LORD, kept a record of sins, O Lord, who could stand? But with you there is forgiveness" (Psalm 130:3,4). I might add that someone who is suicidal is not typically thinking about heaven. He is thinking about how he may find relief for his pain. Our reason for speaking the gospel to him is to offer relief. If we can reassure him that he is still God's child, God willing, we may reduce the intensity of the hopelessness he is feeling and his desire to escape life.

The truth will surely prove ironic. We refrain from telling the suicidal person that suicide can only lead to hell. We assure him that there is forgiveness for the believer despite what he is feeling, thinking, or even speculating. We point him to the Lamb of God "who takes away the sin of the world!" (John 1:29). Only then, perhaps, after having believed that all is hopeless, will he experience enough relief so that he no longer wishes to pursue suicide.

The Need for Gospel Relief

There is an alternative to shaming the hopeless into silence by calling attention to his most disturbing thoughts. You can try to remove a segment of shame—be it ever so small—by asking him to talk to you concerning the pain that is tormenting him. Then present to him the consoling message of Christ. Remember the words of the apostle, "Now instead, you ought to forgive and comfort him, so that he will not be overwhelmed by excessive sorrow. I urge you, therefore, to reaffirm your love for him" (2 Corinthians 2:7,8). Instead of shaming the one who is already ashamed, assure this brother or sister of the grace of our Savior. And do not stop after one affirmation. The clinically depressed or suicidal may need to hear a confirmation of God's love almost continually.

The message of the gospel also gives the hopeless a reason for living. Consider the apostle's successful attempt at suicide prevention in Philippi (Acts 16). Paul and Silas had been flogged and thrown into jail for speaking in the name of Christ. Their stay was apparently short lived when at midnight the foundations of the prison were shaken by a violent earthquake. All at once the prison doors flew open and everyone's chains were loosened. Observing that the prisoners had an instant ticket to freedom, the jailer drew his sword with the intention of killing himself. What was Paul's reaction? Did he speak law or gospel? Actually, the law is what prompted the jailer's desire to end his life. Roman law mandated that the jailer undergo the same punishment as the malefactors who escaped. Death was inevitable, and the jailer concluded that death by suicide was better than disgrace. As it was, the apostle would not exercise the law to rescue the jailer from tragedy. He did not advise the man that unless he reconsidered his sinful course, he would soon answer to God for it. Rather, the apostle gave him the gospel. He informed the jailer that his life was not over but God was in complete control of the matter. "Don't harm yourself!" he said to the man. "We are all here!" (Acts 16:28). The jailer received immediate assurance that the life he presumed was hopeless was very much on track. Despite the earthquake and the open cell doors, the prisoners had remained in their cells.

That, of course, was just the beginning of what St. Paul related to this man. Note what the apostle then said when the jailer who had nearly ended his life expressed his desire to be saved. Paul did not talk about the man's brief desire to commit suicide. He did not shame the jailer for having considered what would have brought absolute disaster upon himself and his entire family. Paul and Silas simply told him, "Believe in the Lord Jesus, and you will be saved—you and your household" (Acts 16:31). There was no need at this point for the jailer to hear the accusations of the law. He needed the assurance that only the gospel could supply. Even when every sector of life appeared dismal at best, the most important truth remained unchanged. The God who gives life and keeps us under his protection and care also forgives and saves us through his Son.

Likewise, talk to the parishioner about what has not changed. Christ bore the penalty of all sin when crucified on the cross so that we, sorrowing sinners, may not fear God's wrath and punishment. The punishment "that brought us peace was upon him" Isaiah remarked (53:5). In Christ there is peace and safety through his death and resurrection. Tell the Christian, "There are only two places your sin can rest in the end, on Christ or on yourself. If through faith your sins rest on Christ, there is no punishment and you have nothing to fear. Christ's suffering is complete, and neither you nor I can add anything to it."

Under the cross

There is a question, of course, that may surface at this point for the Christian who lacks hope. "If God has punished his Son in my place, why am I suffering in this way?" Speaking the gospel to the hopeless can generate a troubling paradox as he reflects upon his beliefs, on the one hand, and his experiences, on the other. The same God who has the power to save him from his sin apparently does not have the power to rescue him from his *suffering*. "If my Lord is willing to die for me to save me from eternal damnation, why doesn't he rescue me from my *current* hell?"

There are three things to consider when consoling those who suffer under the cross of hopelessness. First, do not be afraid to confirm to the parishioner that every Christian must live under a cross. Second, beware of a tendency among some clergy to conceal the cross. And, third, be mindful of the opposite extreme of magnifying the cross.

To live as a Christian in our fallen world is to live under the cross. Not only do we expect persecution from the world at large, which despises the gospel, in a broader sense, we expect to be plagued by sin and its consequences. Assure the troubled believer that affliction and grief result when we are forced to deal with illness and other life-changing events. His cross is not an indication that God is punishing him. The feeling of uselessness is not a sign that God no longer has any purpose for him. It is not that God lacks the power to relieve his suffering. Since he is a Christian, however, he may have a cross to bear for a time. A cross is any kind of suffering brought upon the believer by the devil in particular or by life in general since we live in a world that is utterly affected by sin. God uses *our* crosses in order to put us in touch with our *Savior's* cross. His purpose is to destroy the confidence we have in ourselves so that we may place our confidence in God. We are strengthened in our faith when a given cross directs us to God's Word and our Savior, who has rescued us from the wages of sin.

Even if we understand the purpose of a cross, however, that is not to say that others will always be able to relate to our cross or support us in our distress. Often the most severe cross we are given to carry, in fact, is the cross that others have trouble comprehending and which we must therefore endure alone. So was the suffering of our Lord Jesus, to be sure. The night before his crucifixion, he said to his disciples, "My soul is overwhelmed with sorrow to the point of death. Stay here and keep watch with me" (Matthew 26:38). But the disciples, being the flawed humans they were, fell asleep instead. They would not even *attempt* to identify with the crushing burden that had been placed upon their Lord. Although they were the only ones who might possibly have offered some encouragement to Christ in his hour of need, they chose instead the quickest method of escape. Jesus consequently was on his own and would have to pray by himself. "My Father, if it is not possible for this cup to be taken away unless I drink it" he prayed, "may your will be done" (Matthew 26:42).

Living with a cross does not mean making sense of our crosses. On the one hand, God may require that we live with this paradox that harasses us, offering no explanation as to why. On the other hand, family and friends may have a difficult time understanding what troubles us. In both cases, those upon whom we rely the most for encouragement have, for differing reasons, chosen to remain silent about our grief. This is not to say that our crosses serve no purpose. Although Christ's cup of suffering was not removed, he was nevertheless strengthened in his resolve to suffer and die in our place. He would retain his one focus to be our substitute through life and death and save us from everlasting death. Similarly, although the Lord may give no response to our pleas to remove a particular cross, he always has a reason for permitting us to suffer under a cross.

Articulate this as clearly as you can to the hopeless. God has a reason for postponing his relief. He wants to sharpen the believer's focus on God's Son, increasing his confidence in a very important fact. Christ has taken his burdens to the cross that he might be relieved of the miseries of this life. Even if not one of his closest peers or loved ones understands what's behind his continuing distress, he still has what's sufficient as a believer. He has forgiveness and salvation from his God, who *does* understand.

That is why the apostle could actually brag about his cross, which he termed his "thorn in my flesh." He wrote:

> To keep me from becoming conceited because of these surpassingly great revelations, there was given me a thorn in my flesh, a messenger of Satan, to torment me. Three times I pleaded with the Lord to take it away from me. But he said to me, "My grace is sufficient for you, for my power is made perfect in weakness." Therefore I will boast all the more gladly about my weaknesses, so that Christ's power may rest on me. That is why, for Christ's sake, I delight in weaknesses, in insults, in hardships, in persecutions, in difficulties. For when I am weak, then I am strong. (2 Corinthians 12:7-10)

A Christian need not make sense of his cross before he receives *great* reassurance from the same cross. Assure the despairing believer that he can rejoice in his depression, not necessarily in the sense that he feels happy about it and no longer regards it as unpleasant or undesirable but in the sense that it points him in his great weakness to the grace of his Savior.

Concealing the cross

Having said that, there are a couple dangers of which you should be aware when you speak of crosses that Christians may bear. One is to *conceal* the cross. The other is to *magnify* the cross. Pastors and other church workers may conceal the cross by avoiding to talk about the crosses Christians are given, perhaps with hopes of protecting a believer during his current struggle. This is explained, surely, by society's aversion to suffering, which has had an effect on how the church ministers to the sufferer.

The master at concealing the cross is, without a question, Satan. Consider the temptation Christ faced in the wilderness. The devil's objective from the very beginning was to get Christ to question the importance of his cross and of dying for the sins of the world. So he led Jesus up to Jerusalem and had him stand on the highest point of the temple. "'If you are the Son of God,' he said, 'throw yourself down from here. For it is written "He will command his angels concerning you to guard you carefully; they will lift you up in their hands, so that you will not strike your foot against a stone"'" (Luke 4:9-11). Did Satan really care what might serve in Jesus' best interest? I believe he was hoping to offer Christ a fallacious solution to his troubles, as he tries to do for many in the church who despair. Jesus needed a reason for living. And so far it seemed that he had nothing to look forward to but misery, suffering, and death! Satan wanted Jesus to ask himself: "Why should I believe the Father will accept his Son's sacrifice as a ransom for all sin if he can't even accept his Son's plea for protection?" Even so, the Father could prove his faithfulness if Jesus threw himself down. Much like the person who attempts suicide in an effort to test whether his life is still salvageable, Christ should test his Father, demand some *kind* of evidence that his calling as the world's Savior was worth it.

Satan also wages his assault in instances where we have been given a cross. Like Christ, we should know that bearing a cross is beneath us, not something that is suitable in our case. Therefore, we must sometimes test our Father in order to improve life's forecast. To achieve his objective, the devil puts a similar argument to the believer. "If you are a child of God, you can be sure the Lord is interested in your welfare. He wants you to be healthy and sound. For that reason, he teaches you concerning the power of prayer for healing. God, furthermore, wants you to think positive thoughts at all times since he promises to work everything together for your good." So what if things *don't* go your way? Despite your regular and sincere prayers, you are *not* healthy and sound. You are not capable of thinking positive thoughts inasmuch as things are apparently *not* working for your good. What if God in heaven does whatever pleases him (Psalm 115:3) and you have nothing to show for it but misery and immeasurable sadness? According to Satan, you get to fill in the blanks. If you are a child of God, you have the right to enjoy your life without the aggravation of some cross you never asked for. So you can opt out. Get rid of your cross, even if it costs you your life.

Those who propose that God doesn't want us to suffer offer the hopeless person nothing but an excuse to listen to Satan's latest lesson in logic. If in our efforts to comfort the suffering, we do not speak of life under the cross, we are almost certain to offer false hope. People will not learn how to cope with the truth if we avoid telling them the truth. Just as regrettable is the mistake some make by suggesting that since nothing is set in stone, one can expect that God will soon remove his cross. It may seem like the easiest and most obvious way to cheer up the despairing believer. "You don't know things will happen as you've described them!" That may be. However, if he cannot be certain that things will continue to go from bad to worse, how can he be certain that things will go from worse to better? When we argue that future circumstances are never fully certain, we condemn the hopeless to almost certain suffering, by encouraging an irrational hope.[2]

We do not restore hope in the hopeless by pretending that his cross does not exist. A Christian is not one who's learned how to "just say no" to his cross. A Christian is one who trusts in Christ and his gospel despite the effects of his cross. In some cases, a cross may be ours to bear for some time. But we may consider this only a privilege since Scriptures and experience teach us that we are never so well armed against the danger of falling from grace as when we are afflicted and oppressed.[3]

So what shall you tell a Christian who relates to you, "I don't think I can hold on anymore; I can't take much more of this; I think I may be losing my faith"? You are not going to relieve his feeling of hopelessness by offering him a glorified pep talk of sorts or coaching him to hang in there: "You can do it!" The hopeless need to hear God's Word. He needs to hear from you the saving news of the gospel. The best method of restoring someone's hope is to assure him that a person's faith or lack of faith is not determined by whether or not he can beat depression. Tell him God loves believers who suffer. So much does he love the suffering sinner that he took on himself the suffering that was rightly ours. The "man of sorrows" (Isaiah 53:3) experienced every grief associated with sin so that we, with our loathsome rags and all, might stand before God justified!

Magnifying the cross

The second danger is to *magnify* the cross, that is, overstate the importance of the cross and what it achieves in one's life. Many in the church through the years have suggested that one's cross has a sort of intrinsic bolstering affect upon one's faith. The idea is that suffering produces faith apart from our contact with the Word. The truth of the matter is that a balance must be maintained. Those we assist ought to be informed that every Christian can expect to carry a cross of some kind. However, he must never be led to believe that a cross out of necessity has been assigned to him because he is spiritually lacking in some way. Neither should it be suggested that he must endure a given cross for the rest of his life.

So what if it becomes apparent to the one you are seeing that things are likely to remain the same for a while or go from bad to worse? Beware of giving the impression that God may have assigned the same cross to him for life and he is simply going to have to live with this affliction since it is clearly God's will. Such hearsay deserves a blunt response. Imagine what you would think if you woke up one morning with a time bomb strapped to your waist, and there was no hope of removing the bomb without setting it off. Nevertheless, when you talked about dying, people chastised you for your negative thinking and talk. You were lectured that the bomb did not pose any imminent danger for you. Although, in your opinion, it might go off at any time, you should learn to live with the bomb. "Manage the best you can. God's Word will give you the encouragement you need for today."

There is an alternative to criticizing a Christian for his negative thinking. We need to help the depressed distinguish between the cross, with which one is required to live, and that which is life threatening. Failing to do so may prove extremely unfortunate. The person who acknowledges his depression as a cross may do so only as an excuse to avoid seeking professional help. As a result, he may become even more vulnerable to suicide. I am sure you will agree that it is better to have a moaner on our hands than a martyr.

Consider another set of circumstances. If someone were diagnosed with a treatable form of cancer, we would not expect this person to live with this illness that is slowly robbing him of his life. We would find it unacceptable if he stated that God had given him this cross, and with his Lord's help, he simply had to deal with his cross to the best of his ability. If it were terminal, one would have no choice in the matter. If it were curable, however, we would expect him to seek treatment. God willing, radiation or chemotherapy may help eliminate his cancer. Similarly, we ought not expect people to live with major depression if they have failed to receive adequate medical and professional relief. You don't live with depression. You die from depression! Depression is not some delegated assistant of God's, promised to serve the Christian faith. Depression kills! There may be something more crucial than giving the despairing Christian a lesson on the theology of the cross; telling him "this is your lot in life." Say what you can to encourage him to receive needed relief through therapy or medication.

When a Christian's cross receives an improper emphasis and is magnified beyond what our Lord intended, the purpose of the cross is distorted. Pastors who do not choose their words carefully may infer that one's cross will serve as a means of grace, a sort of sacrament through which the Holy Spirit will work faith. If this were so, we might conclude that crosses are to be sought after. However, there is no virtue in suffering. We have joy under the cross not because our cross pleases God, but because our cross is where we meet God and are presented his mercy.[4] Our cross has value but only to the extent that it draws us into the Word. Whenever we are brought to nothing through *our* cross, our gracious God is found through *his* cross.

The Gospel and the Sacraments

Baptism talk

The one who suffers from depression and despair can yearn for what seems like an eternity for relief. But for reasons that remain unknown, God has not provided relief. If a Christian does not see the Lord strengthening him, his grace may seem out of reach. In the end, the person wants to know that he is still a child of God. Despite his sinful fantasies about "checking out," he wants to believe that the Lord will keep him in his faith and in a state of grace. But how can he believe this when his thoughts about dying persist? Sure, he wants to live. But he also wants to die.

The feeling of ambivalence is common among those experiencing major depression. You may observe this as an opportunity to talk about Baptism. The depressed Christian is experiencing more than hopelessness. He is feeling torn between two prospective but conflicting futures. His beliefs remind him that this day is for living and he has a reason to live. But a sense of despair is advising him that death is much more desirable. You may convey to the struggling believer that those in the faith are those who both die and rise again on a regular basis. Let him know that he can live this very day by dying to sin. "What shall we say, then?" asks the apostle. "Shall we go on sinning so that grace may increase? By no means! We *died to sin;* how can we live in it any longer? Or don't you know that all of us who were baptized into Christ Jesus were baptized into his death? We were therefore buried with him through baptism into death in order that, just as Christ was raised from the dead through the glory of the Father, we too *may live a new life*" (Romans 6:1-4). It might be the last thing that would cross his mind at this time. But it is of first importance that he be told this truth: "God promises you a new life, not through *your* death but through the death of his *Son,* Jesus Christ."

Another pastor's words are quite relevant here:

> Dying to live. It sounds strange, but that is exactly how Christ brings life into this dying world through death; his death on the cross. From his body flowed blood and water that day, the signs of his death. But they are signs of life for us. In fact, there is no other way to live than through the death of Jesus. We are all dying; we can either die alone, or we can die in Jesus. But his death brings life, and it is when we die with him that we really begin to live.[5]

The author refers to the two natures we have as Christians: the sinful nature and the renewed spirit of the believer. Through our baptisms we can set aside any ambivalence we are experiencing about life and death. We are permitted both to die with Christ and to live again. It is a daily affair. We die. We live. We put to death our sinful nature. And through the Word of Christ, we are made alive. In Baptism we answer any need or argument for dying by our own hand. We've already died and die every day by God's holy floodwaters. Our vile sins are washed away so that we may live our new lives in him.

In Baptism we observe not only the right kind of death but also the right kind of life. The right kind of death, as just mentioned, is where we die to sin. Our sinful nature, in a sense, has been hidden from

God. The ugliness of our sins is no longer visible to him. The right kind of life, our renewed spirit, is what remains hidden from those who would drive us away from Christ. The apostle said of Baptism on another occasion: "You died, and your life is now hidden with Christ in God" (Colossians 3:3). *Hidden* means "stored up for safe keeping."[6] It is a condition that never falters for Christians. Although every day our sinful nature exposes itself in ways we regret, Christians are hidden from Satan and every evil that would seek to pluck us from Christ's hand. If the devil wants to take us on, he is going to have to go through Christ. Our baptism has the final word on the matter. As the apostle states in our behalf: "I have been crucified with Christ and I no longer live, but Christ lives in me. The life I live in the body, I live by faith in the Son of God, who loved me and gave himself for me" (Galatians 2:20). The final word is also *our* word when we come under attack. We can declare like Luther, who on one occasion said in effect, "When the devil comes knocking on the door of my heart and asks 'Who lives here?' Christ my Savior answers, 'Martin Luther used to. Now I do.'"

The divine service

Whenever possible, I would encourage the hopeless, if they have gotten out of the habit, to start attending divine services. The person experiencing suicidal thoughts needs to be told repeatedly that his perception of various matters has changed. What he believes about himself, and possibly what he believes about the world, has been altered. The divine service can restore both a sense of reality and hope, as those who gather confess together their sin and the Christian faith. As regards our sin, we acknowledge that none of us are righteous before God on the basis of our own acts. We are poor miserable sinners and no one less than another. We all have deserved God's judgment. As regards our faith, the divine service permits us to confess what every faithful Christian believes. Being the body of Christ, we acknowledge what is relevant to the entire human race. Together we affirm not what we may be inclined to believe about ourselves when assaulted by an acute case of depression but what the Word teaches us to believe about our Savior and his forgiveness.

The depressed Christian can sometimes suffer from delusional thinking. Instead of basing his thinking on reality, he bases his thinking on how he is feeling. He feels self-loathing, a sense of worthlessness. Consequently, he believes he is not entitled to the loving and caring attention of others. He may even believe that he is not worthy of God's providential care or his forgiveness. You may tell the delusional Christian that what he believes is not as relevant as what we *all* believe as stated in our church's creeds. True churches of Christ confess a common faith made known to us in our Lord's infallible Word. The teachings of that faith are explicit, plain, and never change. What one Christian believes, therefore, every Christian believes. When as a congregation, for example, we confess that Jesus was crucified, died, and was buried, I can personally believe on any given day that Jesus has redeemed *me*, a lost and condemned person, and purchased and won *me* from all sin, from death, and from the power of the devil.[7]

The divine service is also where God communicates with suffering Christians. This means we do not have to listen to any voice that speaks a different message than what we've already been told through the gospel. Satan, naturally, would have us believe otherwise. We remember how he was hoping to have the last word with Job. He told God that if Job suffered overwhelming loss in life, he would turn his back on God. "He will surely curse you to your face" (Job 1:11). Job's wife later echoed Satan's sentiment, urging Job to "curse God and die!" (Job 2:9). Satan, however, was not given the last word. Yes, God had allowed Satan a long and grueling commentary on Job's life. In the words of his friends, God was exercising his judgment for some hidden transgression. But in the end God would have the final say about his servant. Job's sufferings were not symptomatic of an unrighteous life. Nevertheless, as a result of his sufferings, he would be humbled in God's presence. The suffering Christian of today similarly may be tempted to utter his curses and call it quits. For months or years he may be subjected to a biting speech on his dismal standing before God, the speaker being his illness. Reassure him that despite the unyielding voice of despair, God's Word is irrevocable. He sent his Son to face the Lord's wrath in his place. "Who will bring any charge against those whom God has chosen? It is God who justifies" (Romans 8:33).

In the divine service we seek out God's help. We persist in seeking his relief, even though by every standard we remain sinners. We *can* persist because we have faith in Christ. Teaching us something in this regard is a Canaanite woman who approached Jesus on one occasion. She pleaded with him to have mercy on her since her daughter was suffering from demon-possession (Matthew 15:22). When Jesus informed her that he was in no way obligated to help her inasmuch as she was not of the lost sheep of Israel, she persisted in her pleas. She even accepted Christ's comparison of her with a dog that is entitled to nothing. She stated: "Even the dogs eat the crumbs that fall from their masters' table" (verse 27). As a beggar, she persevered because of her faith. She dared to ask for Jesus' help because her hope was in the Lord's mercy.

The Christian experiencing hopelessness likewise may persevere because of his faith and dare to ask for the Lord's help. It is a primary purpose of the church's liturgy. Despite how deserving we feel, we dare to ask for God's forgiveness in the Confession of Sins because of what our Savior suffered in our stead. We dare to pray in the Offertory that the Lord would give us a clean heart through the words we have heard in the sermon. We dare to ask in the *Agnus Dei* that the Lamb of God grant us peace through his Supper. We dare to approach the altar of our Lord for strengthening through his body and blood in the Sacrament. And we dare to assume in the *Nunc Dimittis* that we may depart in peace. Like Simeon, we have seen our salvation. Having seen the bread and wine consecrated by the words of Christ, we have also seen the very body and blood of our Lord by which he has secured forgiveness for the world. On the basis of the divine service, you can assure the despairing Christian that what he knows about himself, or what any believer knows about himself, is not as relevant as what he knows about God's mercy. Yes, God knows every nasty detail concerning our past. However, he also knows all about the life of his Son, Jesus Christ, who was blameless in the sinner's behalf. That is what matters in the end for the believer. God's mercy is dispensed to every sinner who calls on the name of the Lord. By faith we obtain every right to persist in our pleas for help.

Private confession

It is vital for the depressed believer to hear the gospel and be sustained in his faith. But what shall the pastor do if that person simply will not attend church? He lacks the will to get out of bed on Sunday morning and get dressed. He does not feel that he is worthy to receive God's gifts or to have fellowship with others who do. At the same time, he has made it plain to you that he has been undergoing a struggle. He would prefer dwelling on something other than what he has been duped into thinking as a result of his illness. And you can see that his door is open for you to pay him a visit. Like the divine service, private confession is an opportunity for him to acknowledge what is really wrong with him over what he imagines is wrong because of the admonishing nature of his depression. It is also his chance to hear firsthand that his sins are forgiven. Confession is not the expression of feelings, what we deduce based on an illness, or what we perceive others have deduced about us. Confession is not sentiment. It is admission. Confession is owning up to our sin and in so doing repeating what God has already said to us. This brings David to mind. He acknowledged, "Against you, you only, have I sinned and done what is evil in your sight, *so that you are proved right* when you speak and justified when you judge" (Psalm 51:4). And finally, confession results in absolution. We receive forgiveness for the very same sins we have placed before God.

In every case where a struggling Christian opens up to you, he offers you a wonderful opportunity to declare to him the comforts of the gospel. But do not assume that his confession will sound like other confessions. Instead of telling you specific sins he has committed, he may give you a vivid picture of what's happening inside him and what he believes is wrong with his faith. To you it may be evident this is his illness talking. Even so, listen and accept his confession. More important than persuading him that there is no real basis for his shame is giving him the opportunity to confess what he believes are his failures. He may tell you he doubts God's goodness and power, God's promises and love. He lives in fear and self-loathing, unbelief and despair. You will give great hope and healing if you do not regard the individual's story as a sad autobiography, but hear it for what it really is: a confession.[8] And then promise him what the Lord promises—forgiveness of sins.

We may expect that upon receiving absolution for one's sin, a Christian will return home encouraged and in good spirits. The depressed believer, however, may not feel any better after being told he is forgiven than he did before the two of you first made contact. Again, remind him that what he perceives is not what is most relevant in the end. The parable of the Pharisee and the tax collector can offer some perspective (Luke 18:9-14). First, you have a man who feels quite good about himself. He is not like other sinners. And his actions prove it. Of course, God does not accept his prayer, and therefore what he perceives and feels has no bearing on his status with God. Second, you have a man who confesses his sin, being truly contrite. Note that because of how he felt, he was not even able to look God in the eye, so to speak. However, he went home justified. How he felt was not relevant. What mattered is how God demonstrates his mercy and declares a sinner righteous in his sight. The believer who is suicidal can be told: "God has justified you by faith. That means however foul you may appear to others or to yourself, the Lord regards you as absolutely holy, having no sin whatsoever. For that reason, he has a place for you, his child, not only in heaven but right now on earth in the here and now."

Private Communion

My experience is that the extremely depressed have a difficult time hearing God's Word. They are inclined to avoid occasions where his Word is heard. This may mean staying home from church. Many suffering from depression find it difficult even to open a Bible. For this reason, it behooves the pastor to bring the divine service *to* him. Keep in mind, if he lacks the energy and inclination to participate in the service, he may also be reluctant to accept your invitation for private confession and absolution. In cases of severe depression, the Christian may even lack the incentive to engage in conversation. If so, there still are several things we can do for him. We can read God's Word for him, pray the prayers for him, even sing the hymns for him.

The hopeless individual may lack the motivation to venture out beyond the confines of his home because in his heart of hearts, he lacks feeling. He cannot feel God's love. Though Christ by his blood has redeemed him, a poor and miserable sinner, he feels no comfort. In such instances, the Sacrament of the Altar can provide great relief and support. Tell him: "It is true you cannot see and feel *God* right now. But you can see and feel what he has *given* you. Under the bread is the true body of our crucified and risen Savior, and under the wine is his true blood. His body and blood he gives you for the forgiveness of your sins" (Matthew 26:26-28). You may say little more than this, especially if he is noticeably preoccupied. The feel of the wafer on his tongue and the taste of the wine will speak volumes to his heart. What matters is, he can receive from you peace from a forgiving God, who delivered up his Son for the worst of sinners. And this you provide in God's behalf.

If a parishioner welcomes your visit and desires strengthening through the Word and the Sacrament, it may be in part because he wants a reason for holding on and waiting for heaven. From you, he wants some convincing that he need not precipitate matters by taking his life. The gospel and Sacrament can make the case for you. They are the Lord's means in every case of restoring the Christian's hope in God's faithfulness. Through Christ we have reason to wait in every circumstance for God's relief. "Because of the LORD's great love we are not consumed, for his compassions never fail. They are new every morning; great is your faithfulness. I say to myself, 'The LORD is my portion; therefore I will wait for him.' The LORD is good to those whose hope is in him, to the one who seeks him; it is good to wait quietly for the salvation of the LORD" (Lamentations 3:22-26).

Dealing With a Crisis

When someone to whom we are ministering loses hope, we want to help. If a suicidal person believes his life is no longer worth living, we would like nothing more than to convince him that things are not that bad. Our first inclination, moreover, may be to apply our skills of logic to talk him out of his negative thinking. However, attempting to reason with the hopeless about whether he is thinking clearly and rationally is generally the concern of the trained mental health professional. We have a different task. As servants of God's Word, our purpose is not to renovate the broken. Our job is to lift them up as they suffer under the massive effects of sin in this world. Our job is to administer the gospel. People are brought to faith not because we influence them with clever and impressive words but because they hear the gospel, which is the power of God for salvation (Romans 1:16). Similarly, we do not encourage the hopeless when we demonstrate that we've mastered the art of persuasion. Only the message of Christ can give Christian hope to the suicidal person who is weary and depressed with the burden of sin. My advice to you about offering relief for the hopeless is very simple. Do not determine how you might alter their irrational thinking. Instead, articulate the gospel with its message of comfort and, God willing, offer relief to the person who is considering suicide.

Meanwhile, be aware that some are not capable of listening. Sometimes putting God's Word before the person who is despairing simply adds to the grief he is already feeling. If a person is profoundly depressed, the gospel may not reinforce his faith, but may reinforce his notion that the message is not intended for him. He may argue, for example, "I know God's Word should help me. But nothing I hear offers me any sort of relief. I don't think my Lord has anything to say to me anymore. I am just not worthy of his comfort." It is possible that the person without hope may be *incapable* of absorbing the truth of your words. He may be unable to process the promises of God's Word and apply them to his life.

The importance of listening

It is the temptation of many pastors and skilled church workers in a time of crisis to speak first and listen when we are done talking. Admittedly, if someone speaks of suicide, it is a natural reaction to try to talk him out of it. What is more, we may do so with no thought of how we are coming across. A fellow Christian informs us, "I want to kill myself!" Instead of listening and trying to comprehend where this incredible statement is coming from, we are inclined to answer back with an assortment of indictments: "You don't want to do that! Think of what you are saying. Do you have any idea what your suicide would do to your family? How do you think God would feel if you ended it all?"

There is a danger in doing more talking than listening when visiting with someone who has thoughts of suicide. If we confirm that what the despairing person is contemplating is a dreadful sin, we may shame him into silence. Our speech may make an impression momentarily. For a time it may even deter him from entertaining thoughts about suicide. But we need to ask what our real objective is. Do we wish to judge this person who is seeking help from the church, or do we wish to understand and help? We need to understand what is behind his despair and feeling of hopelessness. Because if we understand, perhaps we then can help.

Let's say a very disturbed Christian comes to you for reassurance. You have some difficulty understanding his real issues, as he appears somewhat irrational. What exactly is troubling him makes little sense to you. Nevertheless, he has come to you for reassurance. He wants to know even as a sinner that he can count on Christ's forgiveness. Rather than trying to doctor his sick mind, your objective may be put in plain words: you listen, you try to grasp what he is saying, and, God willing, you offer relief through the gospel.

The first objective is to listen. If the Christian coming to you is experiencing hopelessness and perhaps thoughts of suicide, listening is the single most important thing you can do under such circumstances. Instead of voicing your opinion of what might happen should he commit suicide, make it your aim to gain information.

This does not come naturally for most pastors. Because of our understanding of Scripture, we have much to say that could prove quite valuable. Sometimes the situation demands, however, that we extend our window of listening beyond what seems reasonable. The parishioner will be more disposed to express himself and give us insight, if he can do so free of interruption, criticism, or being told what to do. So we let him dictate where the discussion is going.

The importance of listening is that you show your parishioner you understand. You can communicate this by summing up what he is telling you. Until you gain his trust, it is a better idea to let him hear, with your assistance, what *he* is thinking than to insist that he hear what *you* are thinking. Convey what you are hearing him say without offering your evaluation on what he is saying. You want to gain as much information as possible while remaining nonjudgmental.

Gathering information may take some time of course. And you may never get a full picture of what is behind his hopelessness. This need not be a concern. Even if you cannot comprehend the nature of his great burden, you can demonstrate empathy for him. You can show that you understand that he is experiencing hopelessness and even despair. You will likely not agree with his understanding of things and his prediction of a bleak future. However, you can demonstrate that you understand where he is coming from, that he believes things will never get better and that is why he wants to kill himself. If you can communicate this kind of understanding, you make it a lot easier for him to listen, in turn, to you and God's Word. God willing, your concern will generate an opportunity to talk about sin and grace. After showing that you understand this person who is hurting from depression and hopelessness, you may get the chance to provide relief through the gospel.

Imagine that opportunity is now. This parishioner has been talking for some time about his troubles. You sense he is willing to listen to what you have to say. You want to keep the door open. What shall you say? Let me first cite a couple things to avoid when speaking to the hopeless. One tendency of pastors and other parish workers is to direct our comments at the illness rather than the individual. We might say, "Things are not as bad as they seem to you right now" or "You'll feel better in a day or two." Doing this will offer a potentially false hope. Do not shame him by speaking to him as one who ought to know of the value of prayer or by arguing that he can too hang on and that God does so care. Instead, speak to him as one whose struggles are real. He may give you a perspective on what it means to feel hopeless and to believe life is not worth living.

Another tendency to avoid is advice giving. For one thing, you may determine after listening a short while that you are not qualified to give advice. To get more specific, do not advise the person who is suicidal that he can change the way he is thinking. The depressed person is often not capable of thinking away his depression. What a relief if he could just repent of what his depression is doing to him and get on with his life. But it is not that simple.

A natural reaction of some pastors if a parishioner mentions self-destruction is *not* to talk about what he is feeling. If he is not *talking* about it, perhaps he will do less *thinking* about it. Drawing such a conclusion would be a mistake. Do not presume that by addressing the subject of suicide, you will encourage him to follow through with some plan. If he has had thoughts of suicide, it may actually prove beneficial for him to speak about it to you. It is likely he has not spoken to anyone else about it. If he believes you are listening and are understanding, he may believe that you can help.

But how will you help? A depressed Christian does not need to be told that it is up to him to make things better (a common belief among those who suffer from depression). He needs to be told that real help comes from the outside. That is where we may inject some unmistakable words of comfort. We help by giving the despairing a reason to express his helplessness. We assure him, "It is not the healthy who need a doctor, but the sick" (Mark 2:17). Similarly, God did not send his Son to those who can manage the effects of a flawed nature and engage in a series of self-help techniques. Christ came to those who are born and bred sinners.

Perhaps you find the kind of meeting I have described so far somewhat frightening. You are afraid if someone shows up in your office one day with thoughts of suicide, you will be at a loss for words. Maybe you are thinking you will not have a lot of empathy when someone talks to you about something as crazy as taking his life. If you have trouble relating to a suicidal person, you may call to mind some words I am sure many of you have incorporated into your preaching. St. Paul says: "For to me, to live is Christ and to die is gain. If I am to go on living in the body, this will mean fruitful labor for me. Yet what shall I choose? I do not know! I am torn between the two: I desire to depart and be with Christ, which is better by far; but it is more necessary for you that I remain in the body" (Philippians 1:21-24). You need not be a despairing Christian to identify with the struggle Paul describes. To believe that Christ has placed us here on earth to serve in our many vocations and, at the same time, to believe in heaven away from this earth is to feel torn. We desire to serve our neighbors. We desire to serve our parents, our children, our spouses, our employers, our employees, and our friends. But we also desire to escape this vale of tears and live with our Savior, which is far better. It is a struggle that no Christian can resolve completely in this life.

The hopeless and suicidal Christian may come to you while undergoing a similar struggle. He is feeling torn. He loves his family, his friends, and his church. But he does not love his life. He does not love being ill or feeling hopeless. To be sure, he would much prefer departing and being with Christ to going on living in the body that promises no comfort or relief in the foreseeable future. You may assure him that St. Paul would understand. You too understand. Like the depressed person, we know what is better and what is our final and promised inheritance. But what shall we choose? Paul did not speak of a choice that he was permitted to make. (As long as we remain in the body, we may only assume that God finds it *necessary* for us to remain in the body.) But that is why Christ made the choice for us by dying in our place. And that is why he rose again the third day, assuring us of his victory over sin and death. By choosing what remains an impossible decision for us, he has made this day a no-lose situation. "If we live, we live to the Lord; and if we die, we die to the Lord. So, whether we live or die, we belong to the Lord" (Romans 14:8).

Getting help

There may be nothing more disappointing for a pastor than to feel helpless in offering assistance in time of crisis. Perhaps you are not able to determine what is causing a person's anxiety and dread. Or, just as relevant, perhaps he is incapable of hearing you and is unable to absorb the comforting assurances of Scripture. Regardless of what you say and how empathetic you may be, you are not able to penetrate the wall of hopelessness that has been constructed by his illness.

In this case, it is not that he needs a refresher course concerning our God, who loves us despite the problems we cause. The hopeless remembers his Sunday school lessons and his confirmation instruction. He stills knows who Jesus is. He knows of Jesus' all-sufficient sacrifice for sinners. The problem is, it does not matter how you explain Christ's most comforting truths or personalize the gospel. In his case it lacks relevance. For many who suffer hopelessness, there remains one pertinent fact. The thought of living holds more pain than the option of dying. Do not be surprised if the despairing does not receive immediate relief from the gospel gems you offer him.

In a time of crisis, you want to help. In order to help the depressed or despairing in a way that can truly benefit him, you may need to make a referral. Even if he is not having thoughts of suicide or does not require immediate help, encourage him to consult with a psychologist or psychiatrist. If you currently do not know someone whom you personally might recommend, consult with other brothers in the ministry about their recommendations. It is important to be ready to assist in this way at a moment's notice. It can be very reassuring to a parishioner, furthermore, if you have an association with the person you are endorsing.

By the same token, it may be apparent to you that the Christian who has come to see you is in need of urgent help because he is suffering from high levels of depression or anxiety and you have concerns about his safety. In this case, it is necessary that he meet immediately with a mental health professional. Avoid using terms that might have a frightening or negative association for him. Instead of making reference to a "psychiatric ward," you may propose making a trip to an emergency room. Perhaps he would consider going with you. Ask him whether you might accompany him to see someone who can help. If you know someone who would be willing to assist in a crisis situation such as this, you might phone him or her and see whether you could meet at the hospital. If the suffering Christian refuses and your meeting with him ends, try to determine what his next course of action may be. If he leaves you and ventures off by himself, it may be time to phone the police. Police officers are trained for such situations. If it is evident someone might be a danger to himself or others, an officer is capable of responding both quickly and effectively.

Conclusion

As a pastor, there is something I have in common with my Christian parishioner. We are both sinners and saints. In the same moment we are both condemned by the law and forgiven by the gospel. Furthermore, it is only death that can relieve us of the agonizing contradiction that we find within ourselves.[9] The despairing Christian takes this truth more personally than the rest of us do. To some extent, that is why death is desirable in his view. It ends the apparent debate between one message, which states that God loves the sinner, and another message, which states that God will not tolerate sin. So, what do we do as professionals when we discern that a fellow Christian knows this only too well and is battling the urge to commit suicide? Part of us believes we can make a difference. Another part of us wonders whether we ought to leave it to the psychologist and other health professionals. What do we do in the end? Shall we offer our help or not?

The real question is whether we believe we can rescue the tormented Christian. Can we help him resolve the paradox that confronts him as a believer? On the one hand, he has been told he is a Christian. By faith he stands before God with no stain, wrinkle, or blemish but is holy and blameless (Ephesians 5:27). On the other hand, he happens to live inside "this body of death" (Romans 7:24), a body that is destined to die inasmuch as it is contaminated by sin. As with everyone to whom we relate God's Word, our aim with the depressed is to help him maintain the proper balance between the law and the gospel, permitting both messages the chance to be heard. If your word does not appear to resolve for him what seem to be competing voices of God, this does not mean you have failed. It simply means that his illness is having a greater impact on his thoughts right now than any message you choose to verbalize. It may also suggest, if he hasn't already sought proper help for his condition, that you assist in this process in whatever way is possible.

Meanwhile, do not give up the chance to articulate the gospel to him whenever possible. As the rain and snow do not return to heaven without watering the earth and making it bud and flourish, neither does God's Word return to him without achieving the purpose for which he sent it (Isaiah 55:10,11). Yes, the ground may get hard and sometimes there is runoff when the rain comes down. But know that the gospel has not lost its power to work salvation for the believer. Despite how loathsome his depression makes him feel, despite his ambivalence, his deflated esteem, his sense of shame, hopelessness, or despair, the message of Jesus Christ and him crucified will still work faith in this suffering soul. God will save him by his grace just as he has promised. He who begins a good work in his chosen "will carry it on to completion until the day of Christ Jesus" (Philippians 1:6).

Notes

[1]Walther, *Law and Gospel,* p. 1.

[2]Margaret Pabst Battin, *Ethical Issues in Suicide* (Englewood Cliffs, NJ: Prentice-Hall, Inc., 1982), p. 140.

[3]Theodore Laetsch, ed., *The Abiding Word: An Anthology of Doctrinal Essays for the Year 1946,* Vol. 2 (St. Louis: Concordia Publishing House, 1947), p. 11.

4Harold L. Senkbeil, *Sanctification: Christ in Action,* of the Impact series (Milwaukee: Northwestern Publishing House, 1991), p. 147.

5Harold L. Senkbeil, *Dying to Live* (St. Louis: Concordia Publishing House, 1994), p. 55.

6Paul E. Deterding, *Concordia Commentary: Colossians* (St. Louis: Concordia Publishing House, 2003), p. 136.

7*Luther's Small Catechism With Explanation,* p. 14.

8Beverly K. Yahnke, *When Death Seduces the Living: Responding to Suffering Souls and Psyches* (St. Louis: Bioethics Conference, "The Image of God: Its Meaning and Implications," November 2005), p. 11.

9David P. Scaer, *Law and Gospel and the Means of Grace* (St. Louis: The Luther Academy, 2008), p. 5.

"NO ONE CAN SNATCH THEM OUT OF MY HAND"

SERMON FOR JEAN'S FUNERAL

September 7, 1994

by Rev. Rolf Preus

"My sheep hear My voice, and I know them, and they follow Me. And I give them eternal life, and they shall never perish; neither shall anyone snatch them out of My hand. My Father, who has given them to Me, is greater than all; and no one is able to snatch them out of My Father's hand. I and My Father are one." (John 10:27-30 NKJV)

Today we consider two mysteries. The first mystery is horrible. It leaves us feeling helpless in our sorrow. It's the mystery of an illness we don't understand, but whose awful results are plain to see. Our sister in Christ—a faithful and devoted wife and mother—lies dead at the age of 41, leaving behind a grieving family. If it were a heart attack, or stroke, or some other kind of physical ailment of a more respectable variety, it might be a little easier to understand. As it is, we cannot understand the helplessness she felt; we just don't know the emotional torment. All we can do is cry out our impotent love to her and feel sad. The mystery of her illness leaves us with nothing but sadness and death.

But there's another mystery for us to consider this morning, a mystery which will give to you, Peter, and to all your children, joy in the coming days, weeks, and years. It is the mystery of Jean's election to eternal life. We call the doctrine of election a mystery of our faith, but it's clear enough for a child to understand. Simply put, it is this: Before time began, God held an election. Jean was elected to be a child of God and an heir of eternal life. Only one vote was cast, but God cast it. That made it unanimous. Jean was chosen to be a sheep of the Good Shepherd. She was chosen in love. She was chosen in Christ. She was elected.

This is why she recognized Jesus' voice. She belonged to him. She was baptized into his name, and she heard his voice. It wasn't the voice of a stranger, but the voice of her Savior, the voice of the One who loved her and gave himself for her. Jean recognized his voice; she listened to his voice; she confessed her faith in his voice, that is, in the words he spoke, the words of the gospel.

The gospel told Jean that Jesus knew her. "I know them," Jesus says of his sheep. Not just that he knows who they are as he knows everything else there is to know. But he knows them as one who loves them. He knows them as one who has received them from his Father who chose them. He knows them better than they know themselves. Jesus knows the pain Jean suffered. As Isaiah said, "Surely He has borne our griefs and carried our sorrows" (53:4 NKJV). But more than that, Jesus knew the sin—all the sin—which Jean ever committed. I know them, he says. I know their weakness; I know their disobedience; I know their sin; I know their fear; I know their terror; I know their emotional distress; I know my sheep. And I love them. And I give my life for them.

That's why his sheep follow him. That's why Jean followed him, confessed him, sang his praises and taught him to her children. She knew him as the One who loved her. Naturally she followed him. She knew him as the One whose words gave her eternal life. Of course she followed him. St. Peter spoke for Jean and every other Christian when he said, "Lord, to whom shall we go? You have the words of eternal life" (John 6:68 NKJV).

And he does. Jesus says, "I give them eternal life, and they shall never perish, neither shall anyone snatch them out of My hand." Now pay very close attention to those words. Who gives them eternal life? Who gave Jean eternal life? *Jesus did!* He's the One who has the authority to give it. Jesus not only knew Jean's sins, but he bore them. He suffered for them. He paid for them, with more sorrow, more pain, more torment than Jean ever suffered. He paid for them all. He did not fail to suffer the full penalty for every single one of her sins. He had every right to give to Jean forgiveness of all her sins—he earned it. And with that forgiveness he had every right to give her eternal life. It was his to give. And he gave it. Now who is there in all creation who could take that gift away? No one! Who is there who could snatch Jean out of his hands? No one! Who can lay claim to a sheep of the Good Shepherd? Not the devil. His accusations are nothing but lies when leveled against those whom God has chosen. Not death. Not when it is Jesus who says, "I give them eternal life." You may look at Jean and think today that death has destroyed life, but your eyes would deceive you. It is as Luther said in his great Easter hymn:

> It was a strange and dreadful strife
> When Life and Death contended;
> The victory remained with Life,
> The reign of Death was ended;
> Holy Scripture plainly saith
> That Death is swallowed up by Death,
> His sting is lost forever. Hallelujah!
> (*The Lutheran Hymnal* 195:2)

Jesus said, "I give them eternal life." These are not idle words, nor are they simply a religious opiate for grieving people. These words are the promise of the almighty God-Man, Jesus Christ, who is one with his Father from eternity. These words are the promise of the One who faced death—our death, Jean's death—and destroyed it forever by swallowing up our guilt with his innocence. He is the one who says about his sheep, "No one is able to snatch them out of My Father's hand. I and My Father are one."

I know that Jean's illness and Christ's promise appear to conflict with each other. And the manner of her death is so hard to reconcile with the beautiful picture in our text where our Lord portrays his relationship with his sheep. And so we try to figure it all out. Let me suggest that we stop trying to do that. We don't have to. And we don't need to justify Jean anymore than we need to justify ourselves. We know Jesus, by whose blood we are justified, and she knew him too, and knows him today and will know him in joyous bliss throughout eternity. She knows the One who bore what she could not bear and who faced what she could not face. What the apostle said is true:

> Who shall bring a charge against God's elect? It is God who jus-
> tifies. Who is he who condemns? It is Christ who died, and fur-
> thermore is also risen, who is even at the right hand of God,
> who also makes intercession for us. Who shall separate us from
> the love of Christ? Shall tribulation, or distress, or persecution,
> or famine, or nakedness, or peril, or sword? As it is written:
> "For Your sake we are killed all day long; we are accounted as
> sheep for the slaughter." Yet in all these things we are more
> than conquerors through Him who loved us. For I am per-
> suaded that neither death nor life, nor angels nor principalities
> nor powers, nor things present nor things to come, nor height
> nor depth, nor any other created thing, shall be able to sepa-

rate us from the love of God which is in Christ Jesus our Lord. (Romans 8:33-39 NKJV)

Or, as Jesus said in far fewer words, "Neither shall anyone snatch them out of My hand." Amen.

Appendix 2

Suicide Prevention: Emergency Numbers and Suggested Web Sites

- 911
- 211
  (Note: Many areas of the country have 211 numbers, which are help information lines, particularly for mental health issues. However, not all cities and counties have 211 numbers. Therefore the reader is encouraged to try the number before suggesting it to a parishioner.)
- American Foundation for Suicide Prevention: 1-888-333-2377
- National Mental Health Association: 1-800-969-6642
- 1-800-273-TALK
- 1-800-SUICIDE
- Suicide Awareness Voices of Education: www.save.org
- American Foundation for Suicide Prevention: www.afsp.org

Mental Illness and Its Treatment: Suggested Web Sites

- American Psychological Association: www.apa.org
- WebMD: www.webmd.com/mental-health
- SAMHSA (Substance Abuse and Mental Health Services Administration): www.mentalhealth.samhsa.gov
- The Mayo Clinic: www.mayoclinic.com/health/mental-illness/ DS 01104
- National Alliance on Mental Illness (NAMI): www.nami.org